Life Ready

THIS BOOK BELONGS TO

_____

_____

36 Virtues
for a
Successful *and* Fulfilling Life

NIC BITTLE

I would like to give a special thanks to the Corn Bible Academy faculty, staff, board, and families for helping me identify the thirty-six virtues presented in this curriculum.
I could not have done this without your valuable input.

A special thank you to Marci Russell for your invaluable contribution in crafting many of the supporting stories within these pages. My prayer is that your words will resonate with students, guiding them toward a life of success and fulfillment.

I am deeply grateful to Tim Kuhns, whose inspiration sparked the creation of this book and the vision for this project.
— Nic

LIFE READY
36 Virtues for a Successful and Fulfilling Life

© 2024 by Nic Bittle

All rights reserved.
Printed in the United States of America.

No part of this publication may be reproduced or distributed in any form or by any means, without the prior permission of the publisher. Inquiries regarding permission for use of material contained in this book or for school editions, contact:

    Life Ready
    P.O. Box 26
    Corn, OK 73024
    Nic@NicBittle.com
    405-818-6552

Neither the publisher nor the author is engaged in rendering legal or other professional services through this book. If expert assistance is required, the services of an appropriate professional should be sought. The publisher and the author shall have neither liability nor responsibility to any person or entity with respect to any loss or damage caused directly or indirectly by the information in this publication.

All Scripture quotations taken from the Holy Bible, English Standard Version (ESV).

ISBN-13: 978-0-9828713-1-7

Contributing Author: Marci Russell
Editing: Morgen Cloud and Kimberly Lippencott
Proofreading: Kathleen Pothier, info@positivelyproofed.com
Cover Design & Layout: Melissa Farr, Back Porch Creative, melissa@backporchcreative.com

GOLD STANDARD PRESS
www.NicBittle.com

Table of Contents

Introduction — 1

Chapter 1: Honesty — 3

Chapter 2: Look for the Lonely — 7
Joe Maur Story — 10

Chapter 3: Choose Joy — 11
That's Good — 14

Chapter 4: Be Dependable — 19

Chapter 5: Value Others — 23

Chapter 6: Do Hard Things — 27
Be Resilient — 31

Chapter 7: Be Prepared — 35

Chapter 8: Think Before Speaking — 39
Humble, Hungry, & Smart — 42

Chapter 9: Be Curious, Not Judgmental — 47

Chapter 10: Choose Your Friends Wisely — 51

Chapter 11: Be Disciplined — 55
The Battle for Your Time — 58

Chapter 12: Take Initiative — 65

Chapter 13: Choose Forgiveness — 69

Chapter 14: Be Willing to Fail — 73
Two Frogs — 77

Chapter 15: Celebrate the Little Things — 79

Chapter 16: Be Generous — 83

Chapter 17: Encourage Someone — 87
The Encouragement Card — 91

Chapter 18: Respect Authority — 95

Chapter 19: Handle Stress — 99

Chapter 20: Be a Stronger Person — 103
Be an *Upstander*, Not a *Bystander* — 107

Chapter 21:	Ask for Help	111
Chapter 22:	Find Your Purpose	115
	Bad Childhood, Good (Maybe Even *Great*) Life	118
Chapter 23:	Embrace Change	123
Chapter 24:	Be Humble	127
Chapter 25:	Be Open-Minded	131
	Ice Cream or Insulin?	135
Chapter 26:	Be a Good Listener	139
Chapter 27:	Lead by Example	143
Chapter 28:	Be Brave	147
	Be Brave . . . But for Whom?	151
Chapter 29:	Develop Self-Control	155
Chapter 30:	Choose God's Way	159
	Be Thankful for Unanswered Prayers	162
Chapter 31:	Build Better Relationships	167
Chapter 32:	Take Pride in What You Do	171
Chapter 33:	Ask Yourself the Right Questions	175
	Daring Dreams vs. Daydreams	177
Chapter 34:	Find a Mentor	183
Chapter 35:	Invest in Yourself	187
Chapter 36:	Give Something Back	191
	What *Really* Matters	195

Final Thoughts 199

About the Author *201*

Introduction

The pace of change in our world is relentless, accelerating with each passing year. Every day brings fresh technological innovations to the marketplace, reshaping how businesses operate. While the world undergoes this rapid transformation, one thing remains constant: the importance of human connections. In an era where artificial intelligence (AI) seeks dominion, relationships are king.

This book presents thirty-six virtues to distinguish you and steer you toward a life of success and significance. Individually, these virtues may not appear remarkable and, truthfully, they aren't. The true value lies not in the information within these pages but in the revelations you will gain from your teachers, mentors, and guides on this journey. Read these words, but cherish the wisdom imparted by those who will accompany you. They not only comprehend these virtues, but they have lived them. They have experienced life's successes and failures and witnessed the outcomes of virtuous living.

Utilize the journal pages provided in each chapter to document your journey. Fill them with your ideas, thoughts, fears, and potential next steps. Write down ideas that will push you and sometimes even scare you. Record your dreams and the small nudges from your spirit that encourage you to try something new.

Along this journey, your goals and dreams may evolve. When they do, commit them to paper. Ample space is provided for you to make adjustments along the way.

Keep this book close, always. Someday you'll desire to share the thoughts and ideas preserved within these pages with your children, even your grandchildren. I am convinced this book can profoundly influence your life's trajectory, if you allow it to do so.

You are capable of great things, and I believe God has placed you here, at this precise moment, on purpose for a purpose. He has a plan for your life. I wish you all the success life has to offer. But remember, success is not found on a balance sheet or in an individual's net worth. The success I envision for you lies in crafting a life of significance filled with God's purpose.

CHAPTER 1

HONESTY

"If you tell the truth, you don't have to remember anything."
— MARK TWAIN, AMERICAN WRITER/HUMORIST

Being honest may seem like common sense, but it is not always easy. Honesty is a foundational virtue that underpins all aspects of life. It forms the cornerstone of trust, and trust is the bedrock upon which all meaningful relationships are built. Without honesty, relationships crumble and trust erodes, leaving behind a shaky foundation of doubt and uncertainty.

But what if telling the truth comes with consequences? Is it okay to be dishonest then?

When you choose dishonesty, you sacrifice your credibility and integrity for short-term gain. You may avoid the immediate consequences, but the long-term repercussions can be far more damaging.

If you want to build a solid reputation at school and in life, then honesty is non-negotiable. Even when faced with difficult choices, always choose honesty. It is not just about doing what is right; it is about preserving your integrity and self-respect.

Remember, every decision you make is a test of your character. Do not compromise your values or betray your principles out of fear or convenience. Stay true to yourself and your beliefs, even when it is hard. In the end, honesty is not just about telling the truth, it is about living with integrity and authenticity.

> *"Honesty is the first chapter in the book of wisdom."*
> — THOMAS JEFFERSON,
> FOUNDING FATHER/THIRD U.S. PRESIDENT

Nic's Notes —

There have been times in my life and career when it was difficult to be honest. Recently, I forgot about a very important virtual meeting with a prospect for my business. This meeting was crucial because it would determine whether I would be a good fit for their company. If they chose to work with me, it would mean ten years of business for my company. In my world, this was a Big Fish!

I completely missed the meeting because I forgot about it. An hour later, I realized what had happened and immediately called my prospect. When she asked what had occurred, I desperately wished for a good excuse. I wanted to say, "The internet was down," or "I had the wrong time zone," or even "My dog ate it," but that would have been a lie. Instead, I simply said, "I dropped the ball. I don't mess up often, but when I do, it's big. I completely understand if you don't want to give me another chance. I'm sorry."

Later, she told me that it was my honesty in that situation that convinced them to work with me. Today, they are my largest client. Always tell the truth, even when it might hurt you. It's in those moments that your character will be revealed.

Journal & Discussion

Consider these questions, then journal your thoughts, ideas, and insights.

1. Why do you think honesty is a fundamental virtue in every culture and religion?

___
___
___
___

2. Can you think of a time when being honest was difficult for you? How did you handle it?

___
___
___
___

3. How do you feel when someone lies to you? Why do you feel that way?

_____

_____

_____

_____

4. Are there times in life when you should lie?

_____

_____

_____

_____

5. What kind of reputation do you want to have with others when it comes to your honesty?

_____

_____

_____

_____

CHAPTER 2

LOOK FOR THE LONELY

"Be the bright light for others when their world becomes dark."
— Anthony Douglas Williams, Canadian author

If you want to make a difference, then seek out the lonely. Truthfully, everyone you meet is fighting battles the rest of the world knows nothing about. It is easy, especially while you are in school, to focus solely on yourself. With homework, sports, music, friends, and more, it is like juggling a lot of balls. But amid all this, take a moment to lift your gaze and recognize the lonely.

Look around and notice the kid without any friends. Find the person walking the halls alone and eating lunch by themselves. Often, they won't make eye contact or initiate a conversation. They may withdraw from activities and spend most of their time alone, so you will have to make an effort to see them and recognize them.

When you encounter the lonely, engage with them. Consider how you would feel if you did not have any friends or anyone to share lunch with. How discouraging would it be to always walk the school hallways alone?

Include the lonely in your conversations and introduce them to your friends. Invite them to join you for lunch, even if they might decline. In that case, join them instead. Ask for their name, talk about their hobbies, or their favorite and least favorite classes. Make them feel important; this alone could potentially change their life forever.

There are many hurting people in this world. Through connection, you have the power to positively change someone's life. Look around and seek out the lonely.

By reaching out, you can make a world of difference in someone's life.

> *"The deepest urge in human nature is the desire to be important."*
> —JOHN DEWEY, AMERICAN PHILOSOPHER

Nic's Notes —

You will have many opportunities to look for the lonely in school. You don't have to search far to find someone who feels like they don't belong. While it's easy to focus on yourself and your circle of friends, I urge you to seek out someone who looks lonely. A kind word and a smile are probably the two things they need the most.

I once heard a story about a senior girl who started having lunch with a seventh-grader just because she looked lonely. It absolutely changed that seventh-grader's life. Be the person who has that level of influence on another.

Journal & Discussion

Consider these questions, then journal your thoughts, ideas, and insights.

1. Can you think of a time when you were left out or lonely? How did that make you feel?

_____
_____
_____
_____

2. What are some signs that someone might be feeling left out or lonely?

_____
_____
_____
_____

3. Why do you believe it is important to reach out to those who feel left out or isolated?

_____

_____

_____

_____

4. What are some simple ways you can include someone in your activities and conversations?

_____

_____

_____

_____

5. What kind of positive impact could you have on someone who feels lonely or isolated?

_____

_____

_____

_____

Joe Mauer story and video
www.ThumbsUpForMentalHealth.org
https://youtu.be/g6tLNupgJBs

CHAPTER 3

Choose Joy

*"A bad attitude is like a flat tire.
You won't get anywhere until you change it."*
— Unknown

In life, there are only a few things we can control: our actions and our attitude. Despite the challenges we face, we have the power to choose joy. Our circumstances may be difficult, but our attitude toward them is entirely within our control. This choice is beautifully illustrated in the biblical stories of Paul and Silas, as well as Job.

In the book of Acts, Paul and Silas found themselves in a dire situation. They were beaten and thrown into prison for preaching the Gospel. This prison was not like the ones we know today; it was more like a dark, damp dungeon. Paul and Silas were fastened with chains or stocks, physically restrained and confined. Yet, despite their suffering, they chose to sing praises to God and rejoice. Their faith and resilience in the face of adversity are a powerful example of choosing joy amid hardship.

Similarly, the story of Job portrays a man who endured unimaginable loss and suffering. Despite losing his wealth, health, and even his family, Job remained steadfast in his faith and chose to praise God. His story teaches us that even in the darkest of times, we can choose to maintain a positive attitude and trust in something greater than ourselves.

Choosing joy is not always easy. It requires conscious effort and daily discipline. But by focusing on the good in our lives and maintaining a grateful heart, we can find joy even during adversity. Joyful people are not joyful because everything is perfect; they are joyful because they choose to see the beauty and the blessings in every situation.

Nic's Notes —

Choosing joy is something I must work on every day. It's easy to let our circumstances drive our attitudes, but they are two entirely different things. Even though I've never been locked in prison like Paul and Silas, or experienced the loss and suffering of Job, I am still faced with situations where I must intentionally choose joy. In my career, I travel a lot, and there are often delays and problems with air travel. I could easily get frustrated with missed connections and time away from home, but I have had to consciously choose not to let my circumstances dictate my attitude. I have found that you can be stuck in an airport and be happy, or you can be stuck in an airport and be miserable. The choice is yours.

Journal & Discussion

Consider these questions, then journal your thoughts, ideas, and insights.

1. Why do you think it is important to choose joy in all things?

___

___

___

___

2. What are the dangers of waiting until life gets better to choose to be happy?

___

___

___

___

3. Whom do you know that always chooses joy regardless of their circumstances? What can you learn from them?

___

___

___

___

4. Have you ever been around someone who is always miserable? How did they make you feel?

___

5. How does choosing joy affect your relationships in a positive way?

___

That's Good:
Finding the Positive in Every Challenge

What determines what is good or bad? Sometimes it's fairly obvious. Getting an "A" on a test, earning the starting position on the basketball team, or getting your dream summer job are all good things. Conversely, wrecking your new car, getting dumped by your girlfriend, or getting fired from your job, those are bad, right? Maybe, but maybe not. We are automatically conditioned to think circumstances are bad once they get challenging or go off track. But could that challenge be considered differently — even good — if you had a different outlook?

Perspective is the way we mentally view things, and it can drastically change how we perceive challenges and even failures in our lives.

One great lesson on this comes from John "Jocko" Willink, Jr., a retired lieutenant commander in the U.S. Navy SEALs and owner of a well-known leadership consulting firm. Jocko tells a story of a subordinate coming up to him and reporting an issue. After listening to the problem, Jocko responded as he always does by simply stating, "That's good." Frustrated, the subordinate finally asked Jocko why he always said that to him when, from his perspective, things clearly were not good. Jocko replied, "Even when things are bad, there is always some good. Didn't get the promotion you wanted? Good. Now you have more time to get better. Got injured? Good. Time to get stronger. Had a failure? Good. You learned something. Unexpected problems? Good. You have the opportunity to figure out a solution. When things start to go bad, don't get frustrated, startled, or bummed out. If you can say the word 'good,' that means you are still alive and breathing, and you still have fight left in you. Get up, dust off, and go out on the attack."

This is an incredibly different take on how to have a different perspective by finding the good within the bad, but it is essentially true. There are always lessons to be learned, experiences to be gained, and skills to be honed that can only come from challenging situations. Thomas Edison, America's greatest inventor and the creator of the light bulb, had an extraordinary perspective on life that greatly enhanced his abilities as an inventor. You see, Edison failed more than ten thousand times before perfecting the electric light bulb. After each failure, instead of getting frustrated and quitting, he kept going. He famously stated, "I did not fail. I just found ten thousand ways that did not work." I imagine him saying after each failure, "Good. I now know that doesn't work," and then moving on until he finally had success.

Having this kind of outlook is not necessarily natural for most people, but it is possible. Consider Winston Churchill. While serving as the British prime minister, Churchill inspired the free world when he defiantly declared, "We shall never surrender!" during England's darkest days. History has shown that he, more than any other person, can be credited with saving Britain from almost certain takeover by the Nazis. Yet, as World War II ended, his beloved country unceremoniously dumped him as its prime minister. Attempting to comfort him, his wife declared that this rejection might actually be good, or a blessing in disguise. "If it is," he replied, "then it is certainly well-disguised."

Despite this humbling rejection, Churchill went on with his life. In fact, the following year he made the Iron Curtain speech, which influenced policymaking in the free world and ultimately paved the way to ending the Cold War years after his death. He also won a Pulitzer Prize, was once again elected as prime minister, and served many years as the elder statesman of the free world.

Even if you are not tasked with leading a nation and winning a war, you can be sure that you will face challenges in life. Jesus warns that "in this world, you will have troubles and tribulations." You will face many rejections, roadblocks, and even land mines in your life. That's good. God allows us to face these challenges to teach, test, or even redirect us. Learn to view your hardships in life as opportunities to make yourself stronger.

Sources:
- Willink, J. (2024). "Jocko Willink." Retrieved from Jocko Socratic Method.
- Retrieved from The Socratic Method, Faith Gateway. (2024).
- Wright, B. "Making the Best Out of a Bad Situation." Retrieved from Faith Gateway.

CHAPTER 4

BE DEPENDABLE

"Half of life is showing up."
— WOODY ALLEN, AMERICAN FILMMAKER/ACTOR

Success in life often boils down to one simple question: Did you show up? It is easy to identify those who are likely to succeed by examining their track record. Did they consistently show up, or did they always have an excuse? You probably know those people who seem to have an excuse for everything and never seem to be there when things get tough. They cannot be relied on to show up for practice or the big game, leaving coaches and teammates questioning their commitment and integrity. If you get paired up with them on a class project, you already know that you will need to do most of the work yourself in order to earn a good grade.

The ability to show up is not just about physical presence but also about reliability, accountability, and trustworthiness. Your best relationships will be built upon the foundation of showing up for others when they need you the most. Can others depend on you, or will you leave them hanging?

In your career, the simple act of showing up can make all the difference. Opportunities abound for those who demonstrate consistency and reliability in their commitments. Employers value individuals who can be counted on to show up, contribute, and follow through on their responsibilities.

Becoming a person whom others can depend on, in both good times and bad times, opens doors to endless opportunities and paves the way for success in all areas of life. So, commit to showing up consistently and watch as opportunities begin to knock at your door.

Nic's Notes —

Technically, you must do more than just show up, but that truly is a big part of it. Show up and do your best, and you will climb the ladder of success faster than you might think. The truth is that the bar is low because many people always have an excuse and look for the easy way out. Most people simply quit showing up in life. If you have ever seen a stream or river cut a path through a rock, then you have witnessed a great example of the power of showing up. I love the anonymous quote, "In the battle between the river and the rock, the river always wins, not through strength but through perseverance." If you commit to showing up every day and doing your best, there is almost no end to what you can accomplish.

Journal & Discussion

Consider these questions, then journal your thoughts, ideas, and insights.

1. Why do you think dependability is an important trait in both personal and professional success?

___

2. Can you think of a time when you were counting on someone to show up and they did not? How did that make you feel?

___

3. What are some challenges you have in being dependable? What can you do to overcome them?

___

4. How can being dependable help you achieve your long-term goals?

_____

_____

_____

_____

5. What kind of reputation do you want to have when it comes to being dependable?

_____

_____

_____

_____

CHAPTER 5

VALUE OTHERS

*"I speak to everyone the same way,
whether he is the garbage man or the president of the university."*
— ALBERT EINSTEIN, PHYSICIST/NOBEL PRIZE WINNER

Valuing others is about treating everyone well and recognizing that each person is important. It is about seeing that everyone is unique and deserves to be treated kindly, no matter their background, beliefs, or opinions. It is not about what school they go to or what hobbies they have. Instead, it is about recognizing who they are as a person.

Think of the impact you could have if you went through life trying to make others feel important. What if you had lunch with the classmate who always eats alone? You don't do this to feel good about yourself, and you may not even view them as your friend. You sit with them simply because you can change their life by doing so. What if you remembered the name of someone who doesn't think you care? What if you treated the janitor like they were the most important person in the world?

Valuing others is not about you; it is about others. Anyone can treat someone like they matter when there is a selfish motive, but that again is about you. Go through each day looking for an opportunity to bless someone else and watch your world change. The late Dale Carnegie, an American writer and lecturer, said, "The life of many a person could probably be changed if only someone would make him feel important." Who can you make feel important today?

> *"Do nothing from selfish ambition or conceit, but in humility count others more significant than yourselves. Let each of you look not only to his own interests, but also to the interests of others."*
> — Philippians 2:3-4

Nic's Notes —

One of the easiest ways to make someone feel valued is to remember and call them by their name. Dale Carnegie once said, "A person's name is to him or her the sweetest and most important sound in any language."

On a recent trip, I found myself talking to a gentleman at the airport who was traveling with his family. His name was Calvin, and I made it a point to remember it. Later that week, I saw Calvin again. When I called him by his name in front of his wife and daughter, they were shocked. You could see Calvin stand a couple of inches taller just because I remembered his name. Both his wife and daughter looked at him a little differently in that moment because a "stranger" recognized him.

When you go out of your way to make others feel important, you not only help them to see the value of their life, but you also create a positive and lasting impact.

Journal & Discussion
Consider these questions, then journal your thoughts, ideas, and insights.

1. Why do you think it is important to value others regardless of their background or differences?

___

2. Can you think of a time when you felt dismissed or that you didn't matter? How did that make you feel?

___

3. What small step can you take today to make someone else know they matter?

_____

_____

_____

_____

4. How does valuing others build better relationships with those around you?

_____

_____

_____

_____

5. In what ways can you show appreciation for others in your life?

_____

_____

_____

_____

CHAPTER 6

Do Hard Things

*"Do hard things,
not because there isn't an easier way,
but because you can."*
— Unknown

You were created to do hard things, to push and stretch yourself. This concept revolves around stepping outside your comfort zone and tackling tasks or goals that may initially feel out of reach.

Successful individuals wake up each day and confront what's hard — kind of like a balloon, believe it or not. While sitting on a shelf, a balloon is comfortable and safe, but that's not its purpose. A balloon never reaches its potential until it is stretched. It is only when a balloon is inflated and stretched, almost to its breaking point, that it fulfills its purpose.

Do you push or stretch yourself, or do you always seek the easy way out? Some people merely do enough to get by, but that's no way to live. Colossians 3:23 says, "Whatever you do, work heartily, as for the Lord and not for men."

In school, what is hard for you may differ from what's hard for someone else. Singing a solo or auditioning for a lead role in a school play might be incredibly challenging for some, while others find it effortless. Pushing yourself to learn a new sport or skill may be easy for some, but it can cause anxiety for others. Really, though, it doesn't matter what other people think of the challenge. What matters is that you do not shrink away from it.

When we do hard things, we grow and become better versions of ourselves. Our resilience increases, and so does our confidence. When life presents a fork in the road, always consider the harder path.

Nic's Notes —

Accomplishing something you will be proud of is rarely easy. That's just how life works. Taking shortcuts in life won't serve you well in the long run. With technology, especially AI, there are more shortcuts than ever before. AI tools like ChatGPT offer new ways to "cheat" us out of doing hard things. For example, I could have written this book in an afternoon with ChatGPT. It might have been easier, perhaps even better in some ways, but it wouldn't truly be my work.

I'm not suggesting that you avoid seeking efficiency. Efficiency is important. Once, I saw a man digging a hole with a large knife when there was a perfectly good shovel right next to him. That's just silly. The key is not to cheat yourself out of the process just because something is hard. Embrace the challenge; the effort and perseverance make your achievements meaningful.

Remember, true accomplishment comes from overcoming obstacles and pushing through difficulties. It's the journey — with all its struggles and triumphs — that ultimately brings satisfaction and pride in what you've achieved.

Journal & Discussion
Consider these questions, then journal your thoughts, ideas, and insights.

1. What are some of your goals that will require hard work and perseverance?

_____

_____

_____

_____

2. Can you think of a time when you chose the hard path and it paid off? How did that make you feel?

_____

_____

_____

_____

3. Can you think of someone you look up to who has achieved success through hard work and determination? What can you learn from their success?

_____
_____
_____
_____

4. Can you think of a time when you chose the easy way out or the shortcut? How did that make you feel?

_____
_____
_____
_____

5. How can choosing the hard path help prepare you for your future?

_____
_____
_____
_____

Be Resilient

"Toughen up! Bounce back! Roll with the punches and keep your chin up!" We hear these phrases often, but how do we truly achieve resilience? How do we develop the ability to endure suffering and "get back on that horse"?

Jesus repeatedly tells us in the Bible that His people will face suffering. It's not ambiguous; it is presented as a fact. Throughout the Old and New Testaments, suffering is an inevitable reality for figures like Job and Paul and an expected part of life for Christ's followers. Look around the world today, or even just in your own living room, and you will see suffering. Whether physical, emotional, or spiritual, all suffering can be used for God's glory.

The following is a true story. However, names and some details have been changed to protect anonymity.

Todd, Renee, and Lena were just three normal kids — eleven, eight, and five years old, respectively. Life was good, except their mom and dad had decided to get a divorce. Despite their father's efforts, he did not get full custody, and the three went to live with their mom in her new rental house several towns away. Before long, their mom began bringing around Jim, her new boyfriend. At first, he was nice, funny, and played games with the kids. But after a little while, he began to ignore them in favor of other recreational activities. Jim and their mom began getting heavily into drugs and alcohol, soon focusing only on their next high.

Living in a house with two drug addicts was challenging enough, but then the physical abuse started. Jim had no patience with the kids, especially Todd. Jim was not shy about using violence as his choice of discipline with the kids, and their mom was either too high or too in love to care, and she was desperate to keep Jim around.

As the addictions deepened, the kids' dad became more aware of the situation. He was trying to get custody, but this meant going back to court, which required hiring an attorney, and he didn't have the money. As time went on, Jim's abuse included their mom, and then he began abusing Renee and Lena in the worst possible way.

All the household money was spent on drugs and alcohol, forcing the kids to fend for themselves. At one point, Todd tried to feed his little sisters by making a paste from water and flour, as it was the only food available. Their father, desperate to rescue his children, started bringing them food and sneaking it through their window. He was able to hire an attorney, who advised him to call Child Protective Services (CPS) to ensure the kids' immediate safety. Once CPS arrived and rescued the children, their father began the process of obtaining custody.

The kids were out of that awful house, but while awaiting the court date, they were separated: Todd was sent to a boys' facility, and the girls shared a room in a girls' facility. Despite their fear and living with strangers, they drew strength from each other and fervently prayed for Jesus to rescue them and reunite them with their dad.

Their father, desperate to bring them home, sold everything he owned, including his home. He couch-surfed when he could and lived in his car when he could not find a place to stay. He saved every penny, and his heart soared when he finally gathered enough money to pay his attorney and reclaim his children. The reunion was sweet, but the kids were deeply traumatized by their ordeal. They had endured months of abuse, starvation, and living amid addiction, followed by time in group homes with strangers. How could they ever "bounce back"? How could they possibly heal from this trauma and grow up to lead normal lives?

It wasn't easy, but they did it. Their dad created a stable, loving, and secure home. He eventually married a wonderful woman who became their mom, providing love and support throughout their teenage and adult years. This new family, deeply rooted in Christ, strove to serve Him and remain obedient in all things. The girls grew up, went to college, married, and had beautiful families. Todd grew up in the new loving home, but he tragically died as a young adult. Even after this heartbreak, the family remained resilient.

If you were to ask these women and their parents today how they survived the suffering, they would attribute it to God's grace. They also avoided dwelling on the past, choosing instead to look to the future. They resisted the temptation to focus on their hardships or call themselves "victims." Instead, they made a conscious choice to focus on others and look up to their Heavenly Father.

Our God is kind and compassionate, especially during our times of suffering. Yet, because of His love, He expects obedience and the ongoing pursuit of holiness from His people, even in the aftermath of terrible events. Paul advised the Philippians to "forget what lies behind and strain forward to what lies ahead" (Philippians 3:13) for the sake of the gospel. This embodies wisdom. This embodies resilience. Be resilient.

Sources:
- Philippians 3:13 (biblical reference to forgetting the past and straining forward).
- Baer, M. (2024). "Make Resilience Cool Again," WORLD news org. https://wng.org/opinions/make-resilience-cool-again-1708392925
- https://www.christianity.com/

CHAPTER 7

BE PREPARED

"Success happens when opportunity meets preparation."
— THE LATE ZIG ZIGLAR, MOTIVATIONAL SPEAKER

Preparation is the key to success. You might not have control over opportunities that come to you, but you do have control over whether you're prepared.

When you are not prepared for a situation, a lot of negative things can happen. Your stress levels go up, your performance goes down, and your reputation takes a hit. Ultimately, your chances of success decrease significantly. Most of us have experienced this at least once before when we find out we have a test that we did not study for. It's a horrible feeling.

On the other hand, when you are prepared, you are better equipped to handle challenges or unexpected events. Murphy's Law states that anything that can go wrong will go wrong. In other words, life will throw you some curveballs, but being prepared makes them easier to handle.

This is essential if you want to succeed in school, music, sports, and life in general. Being prepared is about investing the time and energy to get ready for whatever comes your way.

Choose to be the kind of person who enters every situation prepared. Build a reputation for being someone who doesn't just "wing it" but shows up ready to tackle whatever comes your way. One of the challenges many will face is knowing how to be prepared for the unknown without falling into the trap of anxiety. Perfectionism and fear of failure can greatly contribute to someone's level of anxiety. Being prepared is not about being perfect but simply being your best.

When you make the deliberate decision to be more prepared, that doesn't mean you will succeed at everything you do. There will be times when you still fail. However, preparedness does mean you will have done your part and can leave the situation without any regrets. So, take the time to prepare thoroughly and become known as someone who is as ready as possible for whatever life throws at them.

Nic's Notes —

In my life and career, I have experienced both failure and success. Preparation doesn't guarantee either, but being prepared demonstrates respect for yourself and others. It shows that you care about what you are doing and who you are doing it with or for. Personally, I find it hard to respect someone who just shows up and tries to "wing it." This may sound harsh, but you're not good enough to wing it — none of us are. Invest the time and energy to be prepared, and your chances of success will increase.

Journal & Discussion

Consider these questions, then journal your thoughts, ideas, and insights.

1. Why do you think being prepared plays such a crucial role in one's success?

_____
_____
_____
_____

2. Can you think of a time when you were well-prepared for something, which made a significant difference in the outcome?

_____
_____
_____
_____

3. What are some potential consequences of not being prepared for a task or event?

_____
_____
_____
_____

4. How does being prepared show respect for yourself and others?

_____

_____

_____

_____

5. Can you think of someone who is always well-prepared? What can you learn from them?

_____

_____

_____

_____

CHAPTER 8

Think Before Speaking

"Words are free. It's how you use them that may cost you."
— the Rev. J. Martin, Jesuit priest

Have you ever started to say something and mid-sentence wished you could reel it back in? If you have not encountered this yet, be patient. It is bound to happen. For many, the challenge lies in failing to consider your words before you let them loose. Emotions can often seize control, and then we blurt out the first thought that pops into our heads. Unfortunately, this habit tends to land many of us in hot water.

Here's a quick test to apply before speaking: Is what I am about to say true, kind, and necessary? If the answer is "yes" to all three, go ahead. If not, those words might be better kept to yourself.

The repercussions of speaking without thinking can be significant. Speak something mean and uncalled for, and you may lose a friend. Tell lies, and your credibility takes a hit. The stinging regret from a misspoken word can linger, causing deep and lasting pain. Words have the power to wound deeply. As the saying goes, "A tongue has no bones but is strong enough to break a heart, so be careful with your words." — Unknown author

On the other hand, a well-timed, sincere compliment can have a lifelong positive effect on someone. Kind words spoken aloud can actually save someone's life.

Your words can either be a destructive force or a beacon of hope and encouragement in someone's darkest moments. Choose your words wisely. After all, "how you make others feel about themselves says a lot about you." — Unknown author

Nic's Notes —

The times in my life that I regretted the most were when I spoke without thinking. In my head, what I said sounded funny or insightful, but in reality, those words just hurt others. My problem is that I have been blessed with a quick-witted mind and a clear, articulate tongue. I can craft a witty remark and deliver it with precision. While this helps in my professional speaking career, it has hurt me in the past with relationships I treasure. Just because you **think** something doesn't mean you should **say** it. Run your thoughts through the filter: Is it true, kind, and necessary? If so, you will have fewer regrets.

Journal & Discussion

Consider these questions, then journal your thoughts, ideas, and insights.

1. Why is it important to consider the impact of your words before you say them?

_____
_____
_____
_____

2. Can you think of a time when you spoke without thinking and regretted it later? What did you learn from that experience?

_____
_____
_____
_____

3. How does thinking before you speak build better relationships with others?

_____
_____
_____
_____

42 | LIFE READY

4. How can you do a better job of considering others' feelings before speaking?

_____
_____
_____
_____

5. How can speaking without thinking damage your reputation and relationships?

_____
_____
_____
_____

Hungry, Humble, & Smart

Concepts from Patrick Lencioni's book, *The Ideal Team Player*

Patrick Lencioni, founder of The Table Group, is a best-selling author, speaker, consultant, and fellow believer. He has written several best-selling books, and the concept in this story is taken from his book, *The Ideal Team Player*. In this book, he outlines the three essential virtues needed to be successful in life and on a team. As students, you have likely already spent a lot of time on various teams — from sports to music ensembles to group projects. According to Lencioni, to be successful as a teammate, you need to embody three virtues: hungry, humble, and smart.

Hungry

Being "hungry" refers to having a strong drive to achieve. Hungry individuals always strive to improve and do what it takes to get the job done. They might stay late after practice or arrive early to get extra work done. In group projects, they often carry the bulk of the workload. Simply put, hungry people have a stronger work ethic than those who lack this trait.

In contrast, people who are not hungry often find excuses to leave early or show up late. They might hang out in the locker room to avoid conditioning or skip the hard days of practice. In group projects, their teammates know not to rely on them for much and often assign them the easiest tasks. The hungry do this because if the non-hungry person fails to complete their task, the overall penalty is minimized. Additionally, those who are hungry know they can cover for the less-driven team member if necessary.

Humble

The second lesson we need to learn is how to be humble. Humility means not thinking less of yourself but thinking of yourself less. Humble individuals always consider their teammates. They pass the ball on the court and play in ways that benefit the team. When faced with a difficult shot or an easy assist, they opt to assist. Michael Jordan, for example, claimed he was never concerned about personal stats, only about wins and championships.

Conversely, those who lack humility often look to pad their personal stats. They will take the difficult shot and fight their teammate for the rebound to get another shot. This behavior is not limited to sports. In fact, it applies to other areas of life as well.

However, humility can sometimes be misunderstood. For instance, a player who never takes a shot, despite being the best shooter, isn't being humble. This player is showing a lack of confidence. This person may have good ideas but never shares them because they mistake silence for humility. True humility involves balancing self-confidence with consideration for others.

Smart

The third virtue is being smart, which in this context means being good with people. It's not about academic intelligence or sports IQ but more about emotional and social intelligence.

We all know someone who is very book-smart but struggles with basic social interactions and relationships. They might have an outstanding intellect, but they lack the desire or skill to connect with others on a personal level.

People often excuse this by saying, "I'm just not good with people" or "I'm not an extrovert." While social intelligence doesn't come naturally to everyone, it's a crucial skill for team success and one that can be developed with effort.

Balancing the Virtues

To be an ideal team player, you must possess all three virtues: hungry, humble, and smart. Lacking one or more can be problematic.

- **Humble and smart, but not hungry:** People will like you and appreciate your humility, but they won't rely on you because you're not driven.
- **Hungry and humble, but not smart:** Your team will value your work ethic and humility,

but they will often have to smooth over your social missteps.

- **Hungry and smart, but not humble:** This is the most dangerous combination. You will be effective and well-liked, but you may manipulate others for your gain, making it clear that your efforts are self-serving.

Self-Assessment and Improvement

Lencioni encourages readers to rate themselves in the areas of hungry, humble, and smart. Identify which virtue you excel at, which comes second, and which is third. Then, practice to improve the virtue you find most difficult.

- **If Hungry is your weakest virtue:** Put in extra effort in your activities. Ensure you complete all tasks and help your team finish the work.
- **If Humble is your weakest virtue:** Shift the focus from yourself to your teammates. Spend time considering others' needs and contributions.
- **If Smart is your weakest virtue:** Make an effort to engage with others and show interest in their lives. Ask more questions and consider others before saying what is on your mind.

By being aware of and working on our levels of Hungry, Humble, and Smart, we can all become better team players.

Sources:
- Lencioni, P. (2016). *The Ideal Team Player: How to Recognize and Cultivate the Three Essential Virtues.* Jossey-Bass.

CHAPTER 9

BE CURIOUS, NOT JUDGMENTAL

"I have no special talent. I am only passionately curious."
— ALBERT EINSTEIN

Curiosity is like a key that unlocks doors to new adventures and deeper understanding. So, why do we often find it easier to judge others instead? Why do we rush to assume the worst without taking the time to be curious and ask questions? You might not be this way, but many of us have become experts at passing judgment on everything and everyone, but what good does it really do us? When we judge, we rely solely on our own limited knowledge and preconceived notions, which often leads us to misunderstand what's really happening. It is far too easy to get caught up in gossip or to believe the worst about someone, but what we really should be doing is fostering a spirit of curiosity.

Teenagers, like everyone else, can be judgmental. We can judge others by their clothes, the way they talk, their skin color, or their performance in class or sports. When we do this, we fail to see the real person that God created. We want others to discover who we are without judgment, but do we offer them the same curiosity? If we all crave more curiosity and less judgment in our lives, wouldn't it make sense to be more curious about others?

Being curious means asking the right questions. It is about digging past the surface and uncovering the truth. When we approach situations with curiosity, we open ourselves up to new perspectives and possibilities. We might even learn something valuable or forge new friendships along the way. Instead of jumping to conclusions, let's embrace curiosity and seek to understand before we judge. After all, the world is full of wonders waiting to be discovered by those who are curious enough to look.

Nic's Notes —

I constantly find myself needing to climb out of the trap of judging others. When I notice I'm slipping into judgment, I ask myself, "What do I not understand about this person's life or situation?" This immediately shifts me from a place of judgment to one of curiosity and prompts me to ask better questions. This change in mindset not only helps me understand others better but also fosters empathy and compassion. By seeking to understand rather than judge, I open the door to deeper connections and more meaningful relationships.

Journal & Discussion

Consider these questions, then journal your thoughts, ideas, and insights.

1. Why is it important to approach new situations and people with curiosity rather than judgment?

_____
_____
_____
_____

2. How can being curious help you learn more about others?

_____
_____
_____
_____

3. Being curious will require you to ask more questions. Why is this sometimes hard to do?

_____
_____
_____
_____

4. How can curiosity become a danger to yourself or get you into trouble?

_____

_____

_____

_____

5. Can you think of a time when being curious led you to learn or discover something new and valuable?

_____

_____

_____

_____

CHAPTER 10

Choose Your Friends Wisely

"Show me your friends, and I will show you your future."
— Anonymous

The late American author and entrepreneur Jim Rohn famously said, "You are the average of the five people you spend the most time with." Friends can have an incredibly powerful influence on us. Good friends uplift and motivate us to be better versions of ourselves, while negative influences can lead us astray.

Now, don't get me wrong. It's okay to be kind and compassionate toward those who may struggle to make good choices. However, it is crucial to be mindful of how their decisions might impact you. The key here is "influence." Are their actions and attitudes rubbing off on you in a negative way? This is what we call "peer pressure." According to the Merriam-Webster dictionary, peer pressure is *the feeling that you need to do the same things as your friends to fit in or gain their respect.* If you have ever found yourself doing something you would not normally do because your friends convinced you, you have experienced peer pressure.

That is why it is essential to surround yourself with positive influences — people who inspire you to grow and succeed. Quality over quantity is key. Having a small circle of supportive friends who genuinely care about your well-being is far more valuable than having a large group of acquaintances who might lead you down the wrong path.

Choose your friends wisely. Seek out those who lift you up and encourage you to reach your full potential. Remember, you have the power to decide who you allow into your life and the influence they have on you.

Nic's Notes —

I can honestly say that any success I have had in my life comes down to two things. The first was choosing never to give up, no matter what. The second was surrounding myself with people who inspired me to be better. My friends, my wife, and my mentors have all motivated me to become a better version of myself each day. While I haven't always succeeded in this challenge, the aspiration has always been there. Surround yourself with people who make you better, and never be afraid to inspire others to improve as well.

Journal & Discussion

Consider these questions, then journal your thoughts, ideas, and insights.

1. Why is it important to choose friends who support and encourage you to be the best version of yourself?

_____

_____

_____

_____

2. How can your friends' positive attitudes or behaviors encourage you to become a better person?

_____

_____

_____

_____

3. How can your friends' negative attitudes and behaviors impact you in a negative way?

_____

_____

_____

_____

4. How can you tell if someone is a positive or negative influence in your life?

_____

_____

_____

_____

5. How can you be a positive influence on someone who is not making good decisions?

_____

_____

_____

_____

CHAPTER 11

BE DISCIPLINED

"Discipline is the bridge between goals and accomplishment."
— JIM ROHN

Discipline is a common trait among almost all successful people. They are willing to give up immediate pleasure for long-term benefits. It is not just about handling tough tasks now and then. It is about facing them every day. They go to the gym no matter how they feel, practice music or sports more than what's required, and study hard for exams and complete assignments on time.

Many of us may take on difficult tasks, but we'll usually only face them when we feel like it. When the motivation is there, we tackle hard challenges, but when our motivation fades, so does our effort. Waiting to feel like doing something before actually taking action leads to mediocrity. Great accomplishments rarely come from such inconsistent efforts. Disciplined people, however, always put their future goals above their present comfort.

A verse from Proverbs (12:24) says it well: "The hand of the diligent will rule, while the slothful will be put to forced labor." This ancient wisdom highlights the importance of hard work and perseverance in achieving success. It shows that disciplined action is far superior to procrastination and laziness.

Success is not about how you feel but about consistently working toward your goals with discipline.

Nic's Notes —

Discipline isn't just a feeling, it's a choice. Many years ago, during a conversation with a friend, we discussed the challenge of doing things we knew we needed to do but didn't feel like doing at that moment. Our list included activities like working out, saving money, reading nonfiction books, writing, and investing in ourselves. My friend posed a thought-provoking question: "How would the person you want to be do what you are about to do?"

This question wasn't about how the person I am today would act. It was about how the person I aspire to be would act. This shift in perspective makes all the difference because the person I am today is not the person I want to become.

The late President Abraham Lincoln is attributed with saying, "Discipline is about sacrificing what you want now for what you want most." Reflect on what you want most. Who do you want your future self to be? By focusing on that vision, the discipline needed to achieve it will naturally follow.

Journal & Discussion

Consider these questions, then journal your thoughts, ideas, and insights.

1. What are some long-term benefits to leading a disciplined life?

_____
_____
_____
_____

2. Do you consider yourself to be a disciplined person? Why or why not?

_____
_____
_____
_____

3. What areas in your life could benefit from more discipline?

_____
_____
_____
_____

4. What could happen in your life if you became more disciplined in these areas?

_____

_____

_____

_____

5. Who is someone you know that leads a disciplined life? What can you learn from them?

_____

_____

_____

_____

The Battle for Your Time

The following is a transcript of a TEDx talk by Dino Ambrosi:

If you are currently eighteen years old and live to be ninety years old, you have about seventy-two years left on this earth. More specifically, you have eight hundred and sixty-four months left on this earth. This may sound like a lot of time, but it's really not when you consider a third of that time is going to be spent sleeping. On average, one hundred and twenty-six of those months will go to school and your career. About eighteen will be spent driving, thirty-six cooking and eating, thirty-six doing chores and errands, and about twenty-seven in the bathroom and taking care of personal hygiene. So that leaves you with three hundred and thirty-four months, optimistically, for everything else. So, this is where you tick the boxes on your bucket list.

This is where you pursue your passions and travel the world and leave your mark. How you spend this time is going to determine the quality of your life. But this time isn't just something that you spend. It's also something that you invest. Because what you do with it will quite literally determine the kind of person you become. The body, mind, and character that you will have in the future are being actively shaped by how you choose to use your time today.

So, take a second and ask yourself, what do you want to do with that free time? What things do you want to do that you haven't done? Who do you want to spend that time with? What is worth investing it in?

Now I would be willing to bet that scrolling through TikTok, binge-watching Netflix, and playing video games probably did not come to mind. But today, the average eighteen-year-old in the United States is on pace to spend ninety-three percent of their remaining free time looking at a screen. That is not counting time for school. So, wrap your head around how sad that is. Imagine getting to the age of ninety, looking back at how you spent all your time after the age of eighteen and thinking about all the things you could have done that you did not do because you got distracted.

And I also want you to ask yourself, what do you think over twenty-six years of screen time would do to you? What is that an investment in? How would it change you? It's well established that there's a link between high screen time and mental health issues such as depression and anxiety. But recently we started to unveil the cognitive consequences of excessive technology use as well.

When we're staring at our screens, we constantly switch our attention between different pieces of information. The average TikTok is about fifteen seconds long, and over fifty-five percent of web pages are viewed for fifteen seconds or less. If you're switching your attention every fifteen seconds for an average of eight hours and thirty-nine minutes a day, you are training yourself to become chronically distracted. Think about what that will do to your career, to your relationships, and to your ability to pursue the things that matter most to you.

Unfortunately, the consequences of screen time are not limited to our mental health and our cognition, because every social media platform carries a message that affects what we believe. They influence the way we see ourselves and the way we see the world, purely based on how they are designed.

Screen time often communicates that your worth is largely defined by what you look like and what you do on vacations. It compels you to capture all the most meaningful moments of your life on camera and share them with your entire social network. And it implicitly says that it's more valuable to have one thousand people that will give you transient social approval than a few that deeply care about you, even when it's not your best day. Snapchat inherently says that the quality of our relationships is best measured by the frequency of our communication, regardless of what we're actually saying. You get a point added to your Snapchat streak even if you just send a picture of the side of your face with the captioned streak.

Twitter says that anything worth saying can and should be reduced to an arbitrary number of characters. It says that the world is black and white, that it's more important to be updated about everything than deeply informed about anything. And when you start to compare the messages that these platforms are sending with those of technologies from the past, you begin to get a sense of what we might be losing.

Because the inherent structure of a book says that the world is complex and it takes time to understand. It compels us to walk in the shoes of other people and see things from their perspective with context. And it forces us to focus on one train of thought for an extended period of time, which nurtures our attention. And the letter tells us that our communication doesn't need to be frequent. It just needs to be deep.

So, when you factor all that in, it quickly becomes clear that the opportunity cost of this screen time is impossible to calculate. And I have never talked to anyone that actually wants to spend ninety-three percent of their remaining free time staring at a screen. So, there's a stark difference between how much time we say our screens are worth and how much time we actually give them. And it is critical to realize that is not an accident. That is by design. It's a consequence of a business model that has incentives, which are fundamentally misaligned with your well-being.

Because you are the product that social media sells. These services are free because they are monetizing you. They profit by helping advertisers change your future behavior, whether that be where you spend your time, how you spend your money, or even who you vote for. In order to do that, they have to do two things. They need to figure out which ads are going to influence you by collecting as much data about you as they possibly can. And then they need to show you as many of those ads as possible. No social media is free because you pay for it with your time. Their profit is directly linked to how long they can get you to scroll. And every social media platform is in a battle with each other to capture as much of your free time as possible.

So, let's run a thought experiment. I want you to ask yourself, how much would you pay for your favorite social media platform if it charged you a monthly subscription fee? So, pick the app that you use the most. And raise your hand if you would pay at least five dollars a month. Okay, how about ten dollars a month? Twenty dollars? I don't see any hands anymore.

Well, let's do a quick calculation to figure out how much we're effectively paying for an app like TikTok. We'll assume that you value your time at a rate of twenty dollars per hour. And you're spending two hours a day on the platform, or thirty days in a month. So, you're effectively paying one thousand and two hundred dollars per month for TikTok. So, when you start to do this kind of analysis, it quickly becomes clear that most of us are drastically overpaying for social media.

My ask of you is this. Figure out what it means for you to get a good deal out of social media platforms.

In order to do that, you have to do two things. You have to ask yourself, what value do these services provide? And second, you have to ask, how much of your time is that value worth?

Now I want to be clear that I am not saying social media is without value. It can be an incredibly powerful tool. It can foster relationships. It can introduce you to new ideas. It can even spark social movements. But we need to learn to use it in moderation. Don't let yourself get to the age of ninety only to look back on your life and realize that while you were trying to avoid FOMO (fear of missing out), you actually missed out on living.

That free time is your most valuable resource. Do not give it away for free.

Source:
Ambrosi, D. (2023). *The battle for your time* [Transcript of TEDx talk]. TED.com. Retrieved from https://singjupost.com/the-battle-for-your-time-exposing-the-costs-of-social-media-dino-ambrosi-transcript/?singlepage=1

CHAPTER 12

Take Initiative

"The best way to predict the future is to create it."
— Peter Drucker, Austrian-American consultant/author

Do you take initiative? When something needs to be done, do you step up and do it, or do you leave it for someone else?

There are two different sides to consider when examining initiative, both crucial for your future success.

The first aspect is taking initiative in what you observe. When you see someone who needs help, do you lend a hand? When you notice another person approaching a door, do you open it? Some may see these actions as mere manners or being a good person, but they still require initiative to make the first move.

For example, if someone spills their tray at lunch, do you assist in cleaning it up? In today's world, many would respond with, "That's not my job!" While it may not be a task you're assigned, it presents an opportunity for you to offer assistance, lead by example, and show kindness to others. Proverbs 3:27 urges, "Do not withhold good from those to whom it is due, when it is in your power to do it." This verse is a call to action, reminding us not to withhold kindness when we can give it.

The other side of the coin involves showing initiative in your own life and pursuit of success. This aspect is all about self-motivation.

Are you a self-starter, or do you rely on instructions? In the absence of a teacher or coach, do you waste time, or do you take initiative and fulfill your responsibilities? In many workplaces, you'll find employees doing just enough to not get fired. It is an absolute waste of potential, and these people ought to feel ashamed.

Strive for excellence. Seek out the next step. Look for opportunities to assist and add value to others. You should not need constant instruction, nor should you require permission to do what is right.

Nic's Notes —

In the workplace, initiative is a rare commodity. The ability to see what needs to be done and then do it without being asked will get you noticed faster than almost anything else. It sounds so simple, but our laziness and fear of stepping outside the norm can hold us back. Many people are wired to only do what they are asked. Don't be lazy, and don't be afraid. Dare to be different and take initiative in everything you do. By doing so, you not only set yourself apart but also inspire others to rise above mediocrity. Taking initiative creates a culture of proactive problem-solving and continuous improvement, leading to greater success for everyone involved.

Journal & Discussion

Consider these questions, then journal your thoughts, ideas, and insights.

1. Why do you think taking initiative is important in achieving your personal goals?

_____

_____

_____

_____

2. How can taking initiative help you overcome challenges and obstacles?

___

3. Can you think of a time when you took initiative and it worked out well? Write down that experience.

___

4. How can taking initiative improve your reputation and your relationships?

___

5. How can you improve at noticing when others need help and then taking the initiative to assist them?

___

CHAPTER 13

Choose Forgiveness

*"Unforgiveness is like drinking poison
and waiting for the other person to die."*
— Many people claim to have said this.

Making mistakes is a part of life. You are bound to mess up, hurt someone's feelings, or have things go wrong despite your best efforts. Striving for perfection is a pointless pursuit. Truly, no one can achieve it. The real solution lies in forgiveness and moving forward.

Forgiveness is not only for others. There will be moments when you will need to extend forgiveness to yourself. Maybe you will slip up or make a judgment error; you will find yourself trapped by your own self-criticism until you grant yourself forgiveness.

In other instances, you will find yourself on the receiving end of wrongdoing. You might experience betrayal, hurt, unfair treatment, or even abuse. Despite the pain, it is crucial to forgive — not necessarily for the other person's sake, but for your own well-being. We have all been mistreated at some point in our lives. While holding onto grudges, nurturing hate, or seeking vengeance may seem justified, they only serve to harm you in the long run. Learning to let go and forgive, both yourself and others, is essential to living a happy and fruitful life.

By embracing forgiveness, you free yourself from the burden of carrying resentment and anger. It's a powerful act of self-love and liberation. While forgiveness may not always come easily, it's a skill worth developing for a happier and more fulfilling life. So, remember to forgive yourself, forgive others, and embrace the healing power of letting go.

> *"Be kind to one another, tenderhearted,*
> *forgiving one another,*
> *as God in Christ forgave you."*
> — EPHESIANS 4:32

Nic's Notes —

Earlier in my business career, two business partners cheated me out of a significant sum of money and my ownership in the business. It's a long story with many variables, but the essence is that I hated those individuals for what they did. I know hate is a strong word, but if I didn't hate them, I certainly wanted to. A mentor and friend made me promise to forgive them. (Remember

Chapter 7 about choosing your friends wisely?) Not only that, but he also made me promise to pray for them every time I thought about them. He insisted that I pray for their success and ask God not to hold anything against them for how they had wronged me. Even now, as I write this, I stopped to pray for them. I didn't like it, but I did it.

You know what happened? I stopped dwelling on everything that happened to me. Over time, I felt the pain and the burden of hate lift from me. It's been years, and still, when I think about it, I get frustrated and must forgive them again. Hate destroys any vessel it's kept in. Moreover, revenge never heals a wound. Forgive those who have wronged you, and then forgive them again, and again, and again.

Journal & Discussion

Consider these questions, then journal your thoughts, ideas, and insights.

1. Why do you think choosing to forgive is important for your personal and professional well-being?

_____
_____
_____
_____

2. Why in the Bible does God encourage us to forgive others?

3. Can you recall a time when you forgave someone? How did you feel after you forgave them?

4. Is there anyone in your life who has wronged you and then you chose to not forgive them? What is keeping you from forgiving them today?

5. By not forgiving someone, who are we choosing to hurt? Does the other person need to deserve or earn your forgiveness?

CHAPTER 14

BE WILLING TO FAIL

*"Our greatest weakness lies in giving up.
The most certain way to succeed
is always to try just one more time."*
— THOMAS EDISON

Anyone who has ever accomplished something worth remembering has experienced failure. The most successful people in the world will tell you that they have failed far more times than they have succeeded in life. Michael Jordan, arguably the most accomplished basketball player ever, acknowledged this truth in his Hall of Fame induction speech when he said, "I've missed over nine thousand shots in my career. I've almost lost three hundred games. Twenty-six times, I've been trusted to take the game-winning shot and missed. I've failed over and over again in my life, and that is why I have succeeded."

The only guaranteed way to failure is to not try. If you aspire to succeed in life, you must acknowledge that not everything you attempt will succeed. In fact, there is a good chance that most of your endeavors will not yield the desired outcome, at least initially.

Failure itself is not the problem. The issue arises when one ceases to even try because of failure. Successful people encounter setbacks but then rise again, make necessary adjustments, and persevere. Mistakes are a natural part of life, and I can tell you right now that you will fall short at some point. You will have ideas that will not work out. However, your failures do not determine your future. Rather, it is what you choose to do immediately after facing failure that matters.

So, learn from your mistakes and ask questions. Surround yourself with those who are willing and capable of teaching you and helping you improve. Be open to trying new things and persist until you achieve success.

American business magnate and billionaire Ross Perot once remarked, "Most people give up just when they are about to achieve success. They quit on the one-yard line. They give up at the last minute of the game, one foot from scoring the winning touchdown. Don't be like most people. Don't give up. Instead, try again and keep trying until you succeed."

Nic's Notes —

Failure is not fun, and I have failed much more than I have succeeded. Yet, within each failure was a life lesson that helped me succeed. Early in my career, I understood this and set out to fail as quickly as I could. Don't get me wrong — I didn't intentionally fail, but I wasn't afraid of failure. A mentor once told me, "Fail early and fail often, for in those failures lie the keys to your future success."

Embrace failure as a crucial part of your journey. Each setback is an opportunity to learn, grow, and become stronger. By facing your fears and taking risks, you open the door to greater achievements and the possibility of extraordinary success.

Journal & Discussion

Consider these questions, then journal your thoughts, ideas, and insights.

1. Can you think of a time when you failed at something but learned a valuable lesson from it? What did you learn?

___

___

___

___

2. Why do you think failure is an important part of success?

_____
_____
_____
_____

3. Why is failure something we try to avoid?

_____
_____
_____
_____

4. Can you name someone who experienced significant failure before their success? What can you learn from them?

_____
_____
_____
_____

5. What steps can you take to overcome the fear of failure?

_____
_____
_____
_____

Two Frogs

Once upon a time, on a farm far, far away, two frogs found themselves in a bucket full of cream. The farmer was having a tough time because his cow was not making enough cream. So, he tried to make it go further by adding water from the creek. But in doing so, he accidentally scooped up two frogs.

The sides of the bucket were shiny and steep, and the cream was deep and cold. The first frog looked around and quickly assessed the situation. "It's hopeless," he croaked. "There's no way out." Resigned to his fate, he stopped swimming, relaxed, and soon sank to the bottom, accepting his doom.

The second frog, however, was cut out of a stronger fabric. Determined to keep going as long as possible, he told himself, "I'll swim a while longer. Something might happen." He kicked and paddled and swam with all his might, determined not to give up. Time passed, and he kept kicking and churning the cream.

Hours went by, and the frog continued to struggle. He kicked all night long. When he thought he couldn't kick any longer, he decided to kick one more time. Each time he found the strength to kick one more time. His persistence eventually paid off as his continuous movement eventually churned the cream into butter. With a solid platform beneath him, he was able to rest and then hop out of the bucket and back to safety.

This story illustrates the importance of perseverance and hope. While the first frog gave up too soon, the second frog's determination and relentless effort transformed his dire situation into an opportunity for escape. His steadfastness turned the cream into butter, proving that persistence can lead to unexpected solutions and success.

Don't give up. Regardless of the situation you are in, keep kicking. You never know what is coming around the corner. You never know what God has planned for you. The only way you will find out is if you stay in the fight and keep kicking. Be the second frog.

> *"It does not matter how slowly you go as long as you do not stop."*
> — CONFUCIUS, CHINESE PHILOSOPHER

CHAPTER 15

CELEBRATE THE LITTLE THINGS

"Sometimes, life happens in the little victories."
— AMY MATAYO, AUTHOR

Everyone wants to reach the top of the mountain, but that is not where success is truly found. Success is in the little victories, those seemingly insignificant steps we take every day toward our ultimate goals.

Even though the victories are small, we must celebrate those achievements because it is within these moments that life is truly hidden. So, what little victories can you celebrate in your life?

If you are struggling in a class, a little victory could be completing your homework on time. If managing your priorities is a challenge, a little victory might mean getting to bed half an hour earlier. If health is a concern, choosing a healthier option at lunch today is a small but meaningful win. In sports, small victories could be achieving a faster time on the track or spending extra time in the gym to improve your game. As I write this book, each completed chapter is a small victory that I celebrate. The truth is, if I ignored these small victories, I would likely never accomplish the greater ones.

Success in life is about momentum. A team can learn how to lose just as they can learn how to win. If a team waits to celebrate until after winning the state championship, they might never celebrate because they could lose their energy and momentum. The same is true in your personal life. Strive each day to find the little things you can celebrate. Do this, and the big victories will happen almost without you realizing it. Kara Goucher, an Olympic medalist in the 10,000-meter run, famously said, "Acknowledge all of your small victories. They will eventually add up to something great."

Nic's Notes —

On the wall in my office in downtown Corn, Oklahoma, there's a quote by Ralph Waldo Emerson: "Don't judge each day by the harvest you reap but by the seeds that you plant." Those seeds you plant are the victories you must celebrate. If you focus on planting seeds, the harvest will happen almost by itself. This quote reminds me that success isn't always immediate. Instead, it's often the result of consistent effort and patience. Every small step, every positive action, and every kind gesture is a seed planted for future success. Celebrate these daily victories and trust that the cumulative effect will lead to a bountiful harvest. This mindset not only keeps you motivated but also ensures that you are always moving forward as you nurture growth in every aspect of your life.

Journal & Discussion

Consider these questions, then journal your thoughts, ideas, and insights.

1. Why do you think it is important to celebrate the little things in life?

_____
_____
_____
_____

2. What is a small accomplishment you achieved recently that you can be proud of?

_____
_____
_____
_____

3. How can you help those around you see the small accomplishments they have achieved?

_____
_____
_____
_____

4. What happens if we never celebrate the little things in life?

_____
_____
_____
_____

5. How can celebrating the little things in life help you accomplish your larger goals?

_____

_____

_____

_____

CHAPTER 16

BE GENEROUS

*"Do all the good you can, by all the means you can,
in all the ways you can, in all the places you can,
at all the times you can, to all the people you can,
as long as ever you can."*
— JOHN WESLEY, ENGLISH THEOLOGIAN

Throughout the Bible, God challenges, encourages, and even commands us to be generous to others. In Luke 12:48b, we read, "Everyone to whom much was given, of him much will be required, and from him to whom they entrusted much, they will demand the more."

Although you may not always think it, you have been blessed. It is easy to compare ourselves to others and only see what they have and we do not, but make no mistake, you are blessed. You are also called to be generous. Be generous with your time, energy, and resources.

Generosity is like planting a seed. When you are generous, you will see a harvest. Studies have shown that generosity can have an incredibly positive effect on you. Helping others has been proven to improve your mental health, increase your happiness, and reduce your stress.

Generosity can also improve your relationships by building respect and trust with others. Moreover, giving freely to others creates a positive ripple effect. When you are generous with someone, they are more likely to show generosity to others. Be generous and witness the blessings that flow from it.

> *"The point is this: whoever sows sparingly will also reap sparingly, and whoever sows bountifully will also reap bountifully. Each one must give as he has decided in his heart, not reluctantly or under compulsion, for God loves a cheerful giver."*
> — 2 Corinthians 9:6-7

Nic's Notes —

We all have areas where we can be more generous. I used to wait tables in college and, as a result, I have always been generous with the amount I tip servers at restaurants. Where I struggle is being generous with my time. I often focus on what I want to do with my time, convincing myself that my activities are more important than helping someone else. This is something I constantly find myself needing to work on.

> Although I sometimes struggle, I am constantly reminded that small acts of generosity can make a significant impact, creating a positive difference in someone's day or even their life. Embrace the opportunity to share what you have, whether it's your resources or your time, and watch how it enriches both your life and the lives of those around you.

Journal & Discussion

Consider these questions, then journal your thoughts, ideas, and insights.

1. What does generosity mean to you, and why do you think it is important?

_____
_____
_____
_____

2. Do you consider yourself a generous person? Why or why not?

_____
_____
_____
_____

3. What impact or difference can you have in someone else's life by being generous?

_____

_____

_____

_____

4. How can a lack of generosity affect you in a negative way?

_____

_____

_____

_____

5. Who in your life is a positive role model with their generosity? What can you learn from them?

_____

_____

_____

_____

CHAPTER 17

Encourage Someone

"Never underestimate the power of an encouraging word."
— John C. Maxwell, speaker/pastor

When was the last time you went out of your way to encourage someone or say something kind? Deep down, we all crave a little bit of sincere appreciation or a kind word. It's remarkable how a simple act of kindness can brighten someone's day and uplift their spirits. With all of life's challenges and uncertainties, a genuine word of encouragement can serve as a ray of light, offering hope and peace.

A word of encouragement is like watering a heat-stressed plant back to life. When someone receives encouragement, they not only feel more confident in their abilities but are also inspired to reach for greater heights. This boost of confidence can be exactly what they need in order to step out of their comfort zone and tackle challenges they may have previously not considered.

Moreover, encouragement is a cornerstone of strong relationships. Whether it is with family or friends at school, expressing support and belief in someone's abilities builds trust and strengthens the bond between individuals.

The fear of failure is a common obstacle that holds many people back from realizing their full potential. However, with the right encouragement, individuals can overcome this fear and embrace failure as a stepping stone to success. Knowing that someone believes in them can be a powerful motivator to keep pushing forward, even when the path ahead seems challenging.

The beauty of encouragement lies in its simplicity and accessibility. It costs nothing to offer a kind word or a gesture of support, yet its impact can be immeasurable. Make it a habit to uplift and encourage those around you. In doing so, you will not only brighten their day but also contribute to a more compassionate and supportive world.

Nic's Notes —

My wife, Tarina, excels at encouragement. Everywhere she goes, she tells someone what a great smile they have or how cute their hair is. It's amazing to see the other person's face light up like a Christmas tree upon hearing the compliment or encouraging word.

John C. Maxwell wisely said, "If you think something good, say it." Life is too short to keep all of your encouraging words bottled up inside. Go ahead and make someone's day. As poet Maya Angelou profoundly observed, "I've learned that people will forget what you said, people will forget what you did, but people will never forget how you made them feel."

So, use your words to make someone feel better by spreading positivity and kindness. A simple compliment or encouraging remark can brighten someone's day and leave a lasting impact. Don't hesitate to share the good you see in others — it's a small effort with a powerful effect.

Journal & Discussion
Consider these questions, then journal your thoughts, ideas, and insights.

1. Can you think of a time when someone encouraged you? How did it affect your confidence and motivation?

___

2. How can encouraging others create a more positive and supportive environment at your school?

___

3. Who do you know that needs some encouragement right now? Are you willing to be the person who encourages them?

_____
_____
_____
_____

4. Who do you know that is a great encouragement to others? What can you learn from them?

_____
_____
_____
_____

5. What impact do you think your words and actions can have on someone's self-esteem and confidence?

_____
_____
_____
_____

The Encouragement Card

When my daughter, Elle, was ten years old, my wife and I moved our family to the small town called "Corn" in Oklahoma, population five hundred and three. The first weekend we were there, Elle was determined to have a lemonade stand. She had always wanted to open one during the summers when we lived in Oklahoma City, but I wasn't comfortable with the idea because of the many strangers. In Corn, however, I felt more at ease.

That first weekend, we hadn't put much thought into the lemonade stand, so we simply grabbed some extra cabinet doors from the garage and taped a sign on them advertising, "Lemonade, Sweet Tea, Chocolate Chip Cookies for Sale." In a town like Corn, word spreads quickly, and soon every little old lady and farmer in the county lined up to check out Elle's lemonade stand. Her younger brother, Cruze, helped her, but Elle was the driving force behind this venture. I'm not sure if anyone actually wanted a glass of lemonade that day, but everyone seemed eager to see Elle and Cruze's faces light up as customers paid twenty-five cents for a glass.

The first day of business was a success. The kids counted their money at the end of the day, and they were determined to make the next day, Saturday, even better. After they set up on Saturday, I watched from a distance while catching up on some yard work. Halfway through the day, I noticed that after every purchase, the kids handed each customer a piece of paper. At first, I thought they were giving out receipts and thought, "Great, now we have to start filing sales tax reports on this lemonade stand."

Throughout the day, customers came and went, some of them multiple times, and each time they got a fresh glass of lemonade or sweet tea, a cookie, and a piece of paper. Toward the end of the day, I walked to the lemonade stand with a pocket full of change, intending to support my children's new business venture. I ordered a glass of lemonade and a cookie, and after I paid, I was handed a 3"x5" index card, which I thought was a receipt. As I looked at the card, I realized it wasn't a receipt at all. Written in big letters across the top were the words "Encouragement Card," with a message written below in bright ink.

I asked Elle what this was, and she replied, "Dad, that's an encouragement card. Everyone who comes to my stand wants a glass of lemonade or a chocolate chip cookie, but what they really need is to be encouraged." She had taken several dozen different quotes and messages from various sources and handwritten these encouragement cards. It now made sense why people were coming back multiple times a day. It wasn't the lemonade or the cookies. It was the encouragement card.

Over the next couple of years, word continued to spread about the encouragement cards. My wife and I began to receive photos of people with their encouragement cards. An oilfield worker sent us a picture of his card tucked under his truck visor. An office professional sent a picture of his card tacked on his office bulletin board. Another professional had taken the quote from Elle and included it in the signature line of his email.

A couple of years later, I was writing a book for the construction industry titled *Know This, Do That*. While I was writing the book, Elle asked who it was written for, and I told her, "Anyone who is starting a career, maybe for the first time."

She looked at me and said, "They need encouragement, too, don't they, Daddy?"

"Yes, they do," I replied. Elle committed to placing a handwritten encouragement card in every copy of that book.

I have heard stories about how her random words of encouragement have met someone's need at that particular time with precision. I have seen grown men and women brought to tears by a simple message written by a ten-year-old girl. As of this writing, she has handwritten over thirty thousand encouragement cards that have been delivered all over the world.

You don't have to wait until you have a title or authority to be a person who chooses to encourage others. If my daughter, who started this at such a young age without a title or high-level position, can have this level of impact on others, so can you. I challenge you to think about your reason for not encouraging someone else when given the opportunity. Then, give yourself permission to offer at least a smile, if not a kind word or two.

Source:
Nic Bittle (Host). *People stop for the cookies. What they need is encouragement*, May 7, 2024, [Audio podcast]. Life and Leadership, Season 1, Episode 12. https://podcasts.apple.com/us/podcast/nic-bittle-life-and-leadership/id1732282118?i=1000654786028

CHAPTER 18

Respect Authority

"Respect for ourselves guides our morals, respect for others guides our manners."
— Laurence Sterne, Irish novelist

God has placed people in your life who have authority over you. We all live within a system where authority plays a crucial role in maintaining order and safety. Think about the rules we follow every day: rules against cheating, speeding, and staying out too late. These mandates are enforced by teachers, police officers, and guardians, all in order to keep you and our society safe.

But why is it important to respect and sometimes submit to authority? Shouldn't you be able to do what you want? After all, history shows us that there have been abuses of power. While this is true, respecting authority is about more than blind obedience. It's about understanding the difference between standing up for your rights and simply wanting to do things your own way.

If an authority figure asks you to do something, as long as it is legal, respects your rights, and ensures your safety, it is important to follow their instructions. This does not mean you should never question authority, but it does mean you should do so respectfully and thoughtfully.

Our world is filled with people who put their personal desires above respect for others and the rules of society. Often, these individuals face serious consequences. Learning to respect authority now, while you are in school, will help you develop the discipline and understanding you need to succeed in life.

Remember, respecting authority is not about losing your voice. It is about finding the right balance between personal freedom and social responsibility.

"Let every person be subject to the governing authorities. For there is no authority except from God, and those that exist have been instituted by God."
— ROMANS 13:1

Nic's Notes —

There will be times when you disagree with the authority figures in your life. You will disagree with your parents over curfews and rules. You will disagree with the school administration and your teachers about how you were punished. All of this can build frustration. You will be tempted to scream, "That's not fair!" — and it probably isn't — but remember, life is about preparation for something bigger. It's not about getting your way or being fair. It's okay to voice your concerns but, ultimately, have respect for the authority God has placed in your life.

I prefer to view these moments of frustration as opportunities for growth and learning. Embrace them as part of your journey, understanding that each challenge prepares you for future responsibilities and greater achievements. By maintaining respect and composure, you demonstrate maturity and strength of character.

Journal & Discussion

Consider these questions, then journal your thoughts, ideas, and insights.

1. What does it mean to respect authority? What does that look like in school?

2. Why do you think it is important to respect authority figures, even when you do not agree with them?

___

3. Has there ever been a time when you did not respect authority? What were the consequences of that action?

___

4. What is the difference between respect and obedience?

___

5. Why does God place individuals in authority over us? When is it okay to not follow their instructions?

___

CHAPTER 19

Handle Stress

*"Stress is not what happens to us.
It's our response to what happens,
and response is something we can choose."*
— The Rev. Maureen Killoran

Stress is real, and it comes at us in many forms. There will be moments in your life when it seems like everything is going wrong — you forget an assignment, find out about a lie, argue with friends, or maybe even break up with the person you thought you were going to marry. All of these instances can contribute to a day, year, or even a lifetime filled with stress, if you allow it.

It's important to note that stress is not merely a mental state. It can profoundly affect your physical health, your attitude, your social circles, and more. Often, the instinct is to turn to substances to ease the stress in our lives. After all, it is a lot easier to get drunk than it is to face the situation that is overwhelming your life. This may take away the stress for a moment, but the truth is that we are merely trading one evil for another.

There is no magic solution to eliminating stress from your life, but there are steps you can take. Firstly, give it to God. Release whatever expectations you're clinging to and give it over to Him. Additionally, spend time in prayer and meditation. Step outside, feel the sunlight on your skin, and take a walk. Stay organized because a lot of stress arises from disorganization. And do not hesitate to ask for help along the way; you do not have to tackle everything alone.

And finally, let go of the need to be perfect. You cannot do it all, and you are not expected to. Failure is a part of life, and it is okay because you can always pick yourself back up. When stress starts to overwhelm you, slow down. Take a deep breath and grant yourself permission to be imperfect.

Nic's Notes —

A mentor of mine, Mark LeBlanc, once said, "When your mind is weak, exercise your body, and when your body is weak, exercise your mind." When I am overwhelmed with stress, I first let go of the need to be perfect. Then, I go for a walk outside or engage in some form of exercise. I work up a sweat, then return to my list and complete one small task.

Also, don't be afraid to ask for help from time to time. You don't have to carry every load by yourself. In moments when you feel the stress of life getting the best of you, take a step back, say a prayer, and ask for help. By doing so, you acknowledge your limits and allow others to support you, creating a more balanced and resilient approach to handling stress. Embrace the power of movement, mindfulness, and community to navigate life's challenges with greater ease and strength.

Journal & Discussion

Consider these questions, then journal your thoughts, ideas, and insights.

1. How important is it to recognize when you are feeling stressed?

___

___

___

___

2. What are the main sources of stress in your life right now?

___

___

___

___

3. What steps can you take to reduce the stress in your life?

_____

_____

_____

_____

4. Why is it important to seek help when you are feeling overwhelmed?

_____

_____

_____

_____

5. Whom can you talk to about the stress in your life right now?

_____

_____

_____

_____

CHAPTER 20

BE A STRONGER PERSON

*"Strong people stand up for themselves,
but stronger people stand up for others."*
— CHRIS GARDNER, MOTIVATIONAL SPEAKER

Have you ever found yourself in a situation where you needed someone stronger to stand up for you? Perhaps someone was picking on you and you needed the help of an older sibling or a friend. Did someone stand up for you, or did you bear the brunt of the abuse alone?

Bullies and abusers are often weak and broken individuals. Filled with insecurity, they are cowards by nature, singling out those who cannot defend themselves and inflicting abuse as a show of power. Even though they seem tough, deep inside they are lost, broken, and weak.

Have you ever seen someone stand up to a bully? Have you ever stood up for someone else? Like the opening quote, did God make you a "strong person" to stand up for yourself, or a "stronger person" to stand up for others?

You do not have to look far to find someone in need of help. There are people all around who need a defender. The question is, do you have the courage to stand up for others?

Martin Niemöller was a German theologian and Lutheran pastor who initially supported Nazi Germany leader Adolf Hitler but later became an outspoken critic of the Nazi regime. He was arrested in 1937 and spent seven years in concentration camps, including Dachau. He is credited with the following quote:

> *"First they came for the socialists, and I did not speak out — because I was not a socialist. Then they came for the trade unionists, and I did not speak out — because I was not a trade unionist. Then they came for the Jews, and I did not speak out — because I was not a Jew. Then they came for me — and there was no one left to speak for me."*

Be the person who speaks out for others. Have the courage to draw a line in the sand and say, "No more. Not on my watch."

Nic's Notes —

There have been times in my life when I was the stronger person and stood up for someone else. I can also say there have been times when I needed someone else to stand up for me.

If you want to lead a life you will be proud of, then look for those who are singled out, who are alone and even scared. It can be as simple as standing up for a single person in a time of need. Everyday acts of courage and kindness, like defending a classmate from bullying or supporting a friend facing injustice, can make a profound difference. These actions contribute to a legacy of empathy and bravery, inspiring others to do the same. By standing up for others, we help create a more just and compassionate world.

Journal & Discussion

Consider these questions, then journal your thoughts, ideas, and insights.

1. Can you think of a time when someone stood up for you? How did that make you feel?

_____
_____
_____
_____

2. Why do you think it is important to stand up for others who may not be able to stand up for themselves?

_____
_____
_____
_____

3. What qualities do you admire in someone who is willing to stand up for others?

_____

_____

_____

_____

4. Can you think of someone who needs another to stand up for them?

_____

_____

_____

_____

5. What impact could you have on someone by standing up for them in their time of need?

_____

_____

_____

_____

Be an *Upstander*, Not a *Bystander*

Nate wasn't excited about changing schools. After all, what fifteen-year-old sophomore would be? The good news was that he would still be relatively close to his old school, so he could stay in touch with his friends. The bad news was that he knew nobody at the new school. Nate was a good kid who liked sports, which he hoped would help him connect with other kids and make new friends.

Unfortunately, things didn't go as planned. Although Nate made the JV team, he wasn't exactly accepted by his teammates. He was often excluded from friend groups and their activities. But after some time had passed, he was excited to be included in a team group text.

In December, Nate's old school and new school played a basketball game, and his old school won. Trying to be funny, Nate posted a single letter in the team group text: "W." That little "W" was not well-received and sparked a firestorm of retaliation, which lasted for weeks. Nate received threats from his teammates that quickly spread to other school groups and social media. Someone even took a picture of Nate and posted it online, identifying him as enemy number one, and the cyberbullying continued.

Nate tried to apologize and explain himself, but his efforts only made things worse. His parents noticed he was becoming more withdrawn and self-isolating, but they had no idea what was happening, and Nate certainly was not about to tell them. As time went on, the negative and threatening comments didn't slow down. It seemed like the whole school hated him and wanted him dead. People often said that he should kill himself, that he was worthless, and that nobody liked him. The criticism was constant and cruel.

One day, Nate's father came home from work and did not know where his son was. He started looking for him and went into Nate's room, where he found his precious son. Nate had killed himself.

In the aftermath, Nate's parents spearheaded an investigation with the local authorities. It was determined that more than two hundred students knew about the weeks of cyberbullying and what was being said to Nate daily. Yet not a single person told an adult, certainly not their parents or Nate's parents.

Not one person stood up for Nate or helped him navigate this abuse in any way. They remained silent. After all, some were not participants. They were merely bystanders. They didn't consider that if Nate's parents had known what was going on, they could have intervened and probably saved his life. If just one person had chosen to be an *upstander* rather than a *bystander*, it's likely that Nate would still be alive.

Being a bystander isn't new. It has been an easy way to stay uninvolved for years, even centuries. In the book of Acts chapter 7, the Sanhedrin decided to stone Stephen to death because he was preaching the truth, which opposed their teachings. They dragged him outside the city and began to throw stones at him until he died. While this was happening, Paul (then Saul) held their coats! He stood there while this man of God was stoned to death. He not only did nothing but acted as a coat rack for the ones throwing the rocks. In Romans 1:28-32, Scripture uses the same language found in Acts when talking about being a bystander to sin. The phrase "to give hearty approval" from the passage in Romans can also be translated as "being in agreement by one's presence, being compliant, or serving as a passive or quiet witness."

So, why did nobody speak up for Nate? Why did Saul let Stephen die? Modern psychology may have some answers. There is a phenomenon called the "bystander effect," which says that people in a group are less likely to intervene or help someone in trouble, even if they are witnessing it. This was discovered in 1964 when a group of people in an apartment complex heard a young woman screaming for help. It was late at night, and they were all in their respective apartments while this woman was being attacked. Some thirty-eight people came forward afterward and reported they were witnesses to her cries for help but did nothing. They said they didn't want to get involved and assumed that someone else would call the police. Examples of the bystander effect in today's culture include ignoring bullying or cyberbullying, filming an assault instead of calling 911, or assuming someone else will help.

Simply being aware of this psychological effect is part of the solution. We can counteract the bystander effect and learn to become upstanders by being aware of our tendency to be uninvolved. Secondly, we can empower or prepare ourselves to intervene directly. This might mean standing up for someone getting bullied, or stopping a fight instead of filming it.

While you may not break any laws by being a bystander, there are certainly moral and spiritual ones that we need to uphold. God's Word tells us to be kind and compassionate to one another (Eph. 4:32), serve one another (Gal. 5:13), bear one another's burdens (Gal. 6:2), and love our neighbors as ourselves (Mark 12:31). As Christians, we are called to love and care for one another. We are all made in the image of God, and we are to be His hands and feet. This means we must be willing to get uncomfortable at times and involve ourselves when someone is in trouble. In other words, we must be willing to stand up and be difference-makers. So, be an *upstander* and not a *bystander*!

Sources:
- Acts 7 (Biblical account of Stephen's stoning)
- Romans 1:28-32 (Biblical reference to being a bystander to sin)
- Willink, J. (2024). Jocko Willink. Retrieved from https://jocko.com/
- Socratic Method. (2024). Retrieved from https://www.socratic-method.com/
- Faith Gateway. (2024). *Making the best out of a bad situation.* Retrieved from https://faithgateway.com/blogs/christian-books/making-best-out-of-bad-situation
- Genovese, K. (1964). The bystander effect incident.
- Ephesians 4:32 (Biblical reference to being kind and compassionate)
- Galatians 5:13 (Biblical reference to serving one another)
- Galatians 6:2 (Biblical reference to bearing one another's burdens)
- Mark 12:31 (Biblical reference to loving your neighbor)

CHAPTER 21

ASK FOR HELP

"No one accomplished anything great alone."
— MARK LeBLANC, BUSINESS DEVELOPMENT COACH

Throughout the Bible, great men turned to God for help in their times of need. For example, after God freed the Israelites from Pharaoh's bondage, they found themselves trapped between Pharaoh's advancing army and the Red Sea, facing imminent death. Moses cried out to God for help, and the sea miraculously parted. Later, in the wilderness, the Israelites lacked water. Moses once again called out to the Lord, and God brought forth flowing water from a rock.

When confronted with challenges that seem insurmountable, do not hesitate to ask for help. While you might prefer to figure it out on your own, sometimes it is necessary to set aside your pride and acknowledge that you can't do everything alone.

There is a significant difference between asking for help and simply asking for answers. It is your responsibility to find solutions; however, it is also your teacher's duty to provide assistance when needed. Yet, teachers should challenge you to think critically and solve problems independently, guiding you in the right direction without offering outright answers.

Merely seeking answers without seeking understanding is a disservice to yourself. Do not be lazy. You possess the capability to overcome challenges. You possess the ability to do and figure out hard things. Life will present challenges. One of the primary aims of education is to equip you with the skills to confront those challenges, not just give you the answers so you can pass the test.

Ask for help, not just answers. You're not meant to navigate life's journey alone. God has placed people in your life to support you along the way, but you must be willing to raise your hand and ask for assistance.

Nic's Notes —

It's easy to align with one of two schools of thought when asking for help.

1. For some, their pride keeps them from asking for help. They believe that asking for help means admitting defeat or failure. These individuals have this notion that if they ask for help, they are cheating themselves, and in turn they struggle much more than necessary.

2. For others, when things get tough, they just give up. They ask for the answers instead of asking for help. It's as if they quit trying and

quickly admit defeat. This person doesn't want help, they want you to give them the answers. This mindset creates a lazy and entitled society.

The challenge is to find a balance between pushing yourself to solve problems on your own while not letting your pride stop you from asking for help when you truly need it.

Journal & Discussion
Consider these questions, then journal your thoughts, ideas, and insights.

1. Would you rather ask for help or simply ask for the answer? Why?

2. How can a teacher giving you the answer hurt you in life?

3. What can you learn by figuring something out on your own?

4. Why do you think some people do not want to ask for help at all?

5. Is there something you need help with right now? Are you willing to ask for help?

CHAPTER 22

FIND YOUR PURPOSE

*"The two most important days in your life
are the day you were born
and the day you find out why."*
— MARK TWAIN

It is common to scrutinize ourselves, focusing on our perceived flaws. Equally common is the tendency to compare one's self to others and then feel inadequate. Social media has exacerbated this issue, as it only showcases the highlights of others' lives while masking their struggles. Stories are embellished and photos are filtered, presenting the illusion of flawlessness.

But these comparisons shouldn't matter. Don't measure yourself against others. If God intended for you to possess someone else's appearance or personality, He would have given it to you. He created you as you are with a specific purpose in mind. He requires your unique personality, your mind, and even your nose because He has a plan for your life that only you can fulfill.

The distinctive aspects of your being are not errors but crucial elements of God's design. Don't wish to be someone else; you are already perfectly designed just as you are. Does this imply that we shouldn't work to improve ourselves? Absolutely not. We are called to strive to become the best versions of ourselves.

Have faith that God has intentionally created you for a purpose. He has equipped you with everything necessary to fulfill that purpose. What is your responsibility? Seek guidance from God to unveil His plan for your life, and then follow His direction.

Nic's Notes —

Discovering God's purpose for your life can be challenging, but it is a meaningful journey. Here are a few tips to help you along the way:

1. **Ask Your Creator:** Seek guidance from God by asking why you are here and what His plan is for your life. Prayer is a powerful tool to communicate with God and seek clarity.

2. **Read the Owner's Manual:** God provided the Bible to guide us. Dive into Scripture and seek His wisdom for your life. The Bible is filled with teachings and stories that can provide insight into your purpose.

3. **Focus on What Makes You Different:** Your unique skills and abilities have been given to you

> for a reason. Often, your purpose will align with those things that come naturally to you but may be difficult for others. Recognize and cultivate these gifts.

Journal & Discussion

Consider these questions, then journal your thoughts, ideas, and insights.

1. Do you believe that God created you on purpose for a purpose? Why or why not?

_____

_____

_____

_____

2. Why do you think it is important to find your God-given purpose?

_____

_____

_____

_____

3. What gifts or abilities do you have that are unique to you?

_____

_____

_____

_____

4. What comes easily for you that others might struggle with?

_____
_____
_____
_____

5. Do your purpose and career have to be the same thing?

_____
_____
_____
_____

Bad Childhood, Good (Maybe Even *Great*) Life

Countless stories — from celebrity circles, world history, and even the Bible — recount the lives of those who have overcome adversity. Some of the greatest leaders and entrepreneurs grew up in less-than-ideal situations, surviving broken homes, addiction, abuse, and neglect. Despite these challenges, they went on to lead successful lives and changed their family trees forever.

Winston Churchill experienced a rather sad childhood. He had almost no loving relationship with his father, who was highly critical of him, and his mother, though encouraging, was largely absent.

Ironically, this upbringing significantly influenced his development into the great leader he became. Prone to ill health, with speech impediments including a lisp and a stutter, and an unimpressive academic record, he started schooling at St. George's School in Ascot, England, at eight years old. His physical frailties made him a target for bullies, which perhaps fueled his determination to stand up to mighty foes later in life. Churchill went on to political greatness as the prime minister of the United Kingdom, an influential leader during World War II, and is considered by many the greatest Briton of all time. Churchill's story demonstrates that sad childhood experiences can be overcome and greatness can still be achieved.

We see that a difficult upbringing does not necessarily lead to a difficult adult life, though it often can. There are plenty of examples of this as well. Notorious criminal Charles Manson was born to a prostitute and never knew his biological father. Raised mostly by his mother, who was a career criminal, Manson was already getting into trouble by age nine when he set his school on fire. This was just the beginning of his life of crime, which intensified over the years. He died without remorse in prison at age eighty-three. He will be remembered as a notorious criminal, cult leader, and murderer.

What determines the fate of a child trapped in a bad upbringing? Firstly, parenting matters significantly. People are largely shaped by their parents and home environment. There is no way to measure the importance of a mother and a father to a young child. Michael Cassidy, in his book *The Church Jesus Prayed For*, recounts the moving story of James

Boswell (1740-1795). When James was a boy, his father took him fishing, which James remembered as the most wonderful and memorable day of his childhood. Yet, his father's journal recorded the day as "a day totally wasted." For the father, it was wasted effort, but for the son, it was the highlight of his childhood.

Secondly, sometimes sad childhoods can become springboards for later greatness. Nothing is wasted in our lives. Even past experiences — no matter how bad — can often become the foundation for future greatness. From a biblical perspective, the comforting passage from the book of Joel promises that God "will restore the years that the locust has eaten" (Joel 2:25). In this way, nothing in our lives is ever wasted, and God can use our past experiences — both good and bad — for His purposes.

Finally, we should not let our childhood experiences determine who we become. While they have a huge influence on us, real change is possible, especially when we bring God into the picture. Jesus Christ specializes in transforming lives, taking the most messed-up, beaten-down, and wrecked lives and turning them around.

More than two thousand years of church history provides countless examples of this. No matter what you have gone through as a child, or even throughout most of your life, there is always hope for something better through Christ. No life is so bad that it cannot be redeemed and transformed, even at a late age. In fact, Saul, one of the greatest persecutors of the early Christian church, experienced a life change later on, and he became the mighty apostle Paul. Similarly, God changed the hardened slave-ship captain John Newton into a loving Christian, and he went on to write the hymn "Amazing Grace."

God can change anyone who allows Him to do so. If you have had an unhappy or difficult childhood, it does not determine how you live the rest of your life. Let God come in and turn things around. He specializes in change, and He can take even the most broken sinner and turn them into champions of His transforming grace and power. Romans 8:28 says, "And we know that for those who love God all things work together for good, for those who are called according to His purpose." God can use what you went through for His glory. He is gracious and will redeem things if we let Him. So, let Him.

Sources:
- Muehlenberg, B. (2018). "Great Leaders, Unhappy Childhoods." https://billmuehlenberg.com/2018/01/15/great-leaders-unhappy-childhoods/
- The International Churchill Society, "Winston Churchill." https://winstonchurchill.org/
- Britannica, "Charles Manson." https://www.britannica.com/biography/Charles-Manson

CHAPTER 23

EMBRACE CHANGE

*"Change is the only constant in life.
One's ability to adapt to those changes
will determine your success in life."*
— BENJAMIN FRANKLIN, FOUNDING FATHER/U.S. DIPLOMAT

Do you like change? Do you like it when someone steps into your life and asks you to do something different? If someone restructures your schedule or the coach changes the starting lineup on the team right before the big game, how do you feel? What is your response when a teacher changes a due date or the requirements of an assignment? Most people resist change, but why? The truth is that change is hard, unknown. Even good change is hard.

I love what Winston Churchill said about change: "To improve is to change, to be perfect is to change often." We stumble when we fail to accept the changes that happen in our lives. We try to hold on to what was, instead of leaning forward into what can be. God's plan in your life includes change. As you graduate and leave high school, you will be faced with more change. If you go to college, your home address and your friends might change. If you start a career, your schedule and your priorities will change. If you decide to get married and start a family one day, everything you know will change, and it will continue to change. What's scary is that there is nothing you can do about it, and there is no sense in fighting it. So, you might as well embrace it.

Nic's Notes —

My mother, Teresa Bittle, would often read to her grandchildren a book about Orville Wright and his first flight. This book was not about the Orville Wright you're thinking, the man who worked with his brother Wilbur to invent the world's first airplane. This book, *The Flight of Orville Wright Caterpillar*, was about just that: a caterpillar.

It is a touching story about a caterpillar who dreams of flying one day, but he cannot figure out how God can give him this dream of flight while also burdening him with sixteen legs. He does everything he can in his own power to fly, but he continues to fail. Then one day, Orville feels a change coming in his life, and it scares him. As much as Orville does not like where he is in his life right now, he is reluctant to do anything because change is hard and unknown.

Not really understanding why, Orville builds a cocoon and wraps himself in the dark for what seems like an eternity. Then one day, Orville emerges from what he thought was his tomb and gracefully flies away, beginning his new life. It's really a story of salvation and rebirth. However, when I think about Orville the caterpillar, I am reminded of how much I want to resist change in my own life, even if it's good change. In my experience, I have found that it's best if I just trust God and embrace the changes — both large and small — that He has planned for my life.

Journal & Discussion

Consider these questions, then journal your thoughts, ideas, and insights.

1. What are some changes in your life that you originally resisted but later found beneficial?

___

___

___

___

2. Why is change hard?

___

___

___

3. What mindset or attitude is most important when dealing with change, and how do you develop it?

_____

_____

_____

_____

4. Who do you know that handles change well? What can you learn from them?

_____

_____

_____

_____

5. How can you support your friends or classmates who are dealing with change in their life?

_____

_____

_____

_____

CHAPTER 24

BE HUMBLE

"Humility is the surest sign of strength."
— Thomas Merton, author/Trappist monk

As we've discussed, success in life often involves working with others and getting their help. Whether it is doing well in sports, school, or in your community, teamwork is essential.

So, how can you inspire others to support you? The key is humility.

Humility means understanding that there is always more to learn. No matter how much you know or what you have achieved, personal growth never stops. Embracing this requires humility, being willing to learn new things, listening to different perspectives, and trying new experiences. This is the opposite of saying "I know," which can create a barrier to learning and show others that you are not open to new ideas.

Ask yourself: Are you open to learning from others, or do you think you already know everything? Choosing humility means being ready to learn and grow continuously. This attitude will help you gain support from others and continue to grow. As British writer C.S. Lewis said, "Humility is not thinking less of yourself, it is thinking of yourself less."

Nic's Notes —

No matter how much you know or how smart you think you are, there is always something you can learn from others. My grandfather, Louis O. Bass, was a brilliant structural engineer. He played a significant role in designing the Superdome in New Orleans, Louisiana, and the Astrodome in Houston, Texas. This man literally wrote the book on the use of concrete and structural steel.

When I was young, my brother Brandon and I helped him pour a new concrete driveway. We spent an entire week setting the forms and laying out the steel to his exact specifications, a task that would have taken a decent concrete crew just three hours. But my grandfather wanted it perfect.

When the concrete truck arrived, the driver got out and told us how overdesigned our driveway was. He said it was too thick and had too much steel, among other things. My grandfather just listened. He never told the driver who he was or what he knew. Later, I asked my grandfather why he didn't speak up. His response was, "This guy has driven that truck his whole life and knows things about this job I don't know. I can learn something from anyone."

Be humble. You can learn something from anyone. Embrace humility and keep an open mind, as wisdom often comes from unexpected sources. Your willingness to learn from others can lead to new insights, better solutions, and personal growth.

Journal & Discussion

Consider these questions, then journal your thoughts, ideas, and insights.

1. Can you think of someone you know who is not humble? What is your perception of them as a person?

2. How can being humble help you grow in a significant way?

3. How does pride get in the way of our need to be humble?

_____

_____

_____

_____

4. Whom have you seen that practices humility? What can you learn from them?

_____

_____

_____

_____

5. What small step can you take to practice humility?

_____

_____

_____

_____

CHAPTER 25

BE OPEN-MINDED

"An open mind leaves a chance for someone to drop a worthwhile thought in it."
— MARK TWAIN

Being open-minded means being receptive to different ideas without compromising your core values. Biblical truth is the foundational truth, but everything else is up for consideration.

Open-minded people are typically flexible in their thinking, less judgmental, and show more empathy and understanding for others. But how does one become more open-minded?

Patience with others, their ideas, and their perspectives is a great first step. Be willing to try something new. Getting stuck in a rut with your ideas or ways of doing things is easy. In most situations, different is not wrong; it is just different.

The old saying, "there is more than one way to skin a cat" is truer now than ever.

Another way to become more open-minded is to stop yourself from judging others and their ways of doing things. If you have ever traveled with another family, you have probably noticed that everyone has a different way of relaxing. Some might want to read, others might want to hike or exercise, while still others may want to squeeze every bit of fun out of their vacation by filling each day with plans. One way is not right and the other wrong; they are just different. An open-minded person is open to someone solving the same problem in a different way.

We must respect authority, but we also must respectfully challenge it when the only reason for doing something a certain way is tradition. It was U.S. Navy Rear Admiral Grace Hopper who famously said, "The most dangerous phrase in the language is, 'We've always done it this way.'" Challenge this mindset as often as you can. Being open-minded is a universal need, not just for students. This mindset is crucial for everyone.

Nic's Notes —

A newlywed couple was preparing for their first holiday meal together. The wife cut off the end of the ham before placing it in the oven. Curious, her husband asked why she did that. She replied, "That's how my mother always did it."

Unsatisfied with the answer, the husband asked his mother-in-law why she cut off the end of the ham. She responded, "That's how my mother always did it."

Determined to get to the bottom of it, the husband called the grandmother and asked her the same question. She laughed and said, "Oh, I cut off the end of the ham because my pan was too small to fit the whole thing."

This story highlights the importance of being open-minded and asking, "Why?" By challenging the status quo and thinking critically, we can discover more efficient or meaningful ways of doing things. Never underestimate the power of curiosity and independent thought.

Journal & Discussion

Consider these questions, then journal your thoughts, ideas, and insights.

1. How can you balance being open to new ideas while staying true to your core values and beliefs?

2. How does the secular world want to use "being open-minded" to change your beliefs?

3. How can you respectfully disagree with someone while still considering their point of view?

_____

_____

_____

_____

4. How can being close-minded hurt your influence?

_____

_____

_____

_____

5. What are some questions you can ask others to better understand their point of view?

_____

_____

_____

_____

Ice Cream or Insulin?

"Ice cream is the best dessert."

"Insulin is a medication for people with diabetes."

One of these statements may be true for some, but the other is absolute truth. Absolute truth, as defined by philosophers, comprises fixed, inflexible, invariable, and unalterable facts. For example, insulin is a medication for people with diabetes, but what dessert you think is the best is just an opinion.

Dr. Frank Turek, an American apologist, states that absolute truth is true for all people, at all times, and in all places. These facts remain constant, no matter where you are or who you ask. I refer to this as objective truth — an external fact of the world that is discovered.

Conversely, relative or subjective truth is essentially an opinion and is often called "relativism." Subjective truth depends on the individual and can change. Is ice cream the best dessert? Perhaps for some, but many others might prefer chocolate lava cake, coconut pie, or a pile of cookies and some milk. Some might not even like dessert at all. Subjective truth is not true for all people, at all times, and in all places; instead, it varies with personal preferences. You might hear people say, "That's true for you, but not for me," or use the phrase, "That's my truth," as if truth can be personally owned.

This might sound appealing, but consider trying this at a bank. Imagine asking the teller to withdraw one hundred dollars from your account when she tells you that there's only nine dollars available. You then reply, "That's true for you, but not for me. My truth is that I have one thousand dollars in my account!" No matter what you claim as "your truth," you will be leaving the bank with nine dollars, because you absolutely and objectively only have nine dollars.

Why is understanding this distinction important? Knowing the difference between subjective and objective truth is crucial because it determines what is real, what is moral, and what is good or evil. Truth defines reality. Imagine if words did not have fixed meanings; indeed, communication would be impossible.

Today, we see a growing struggle for truth in society. For instance, if you accidentally bump into a young woman and quickly apologize by saying, "Excuse me, miss," she might respond, "I am a man, do not misgender me!" While she might feel that way, her biological reality, defined by her XX chromosomes, remains unchanged.

So, are things true because we believe them to be, or are they true because they are inherently true? Do you remain on the ground because you believe in gravity? Would disbelief in gravity cause you to float away? Certainly not. Our beliefs do not create reality, but they should reflect it.

What about the statement, "God exists"? Some would say this is subjective, only an opinion. This, however, is an objective statement. Even if someone does not believe in God, it does not change the fact that He does indeed exist. Romans 2:14–16 explains that even those who do not know or believe in God naturally obey His law because it is written on their hearts, reflecting their creation in God's image.

The Bible is not true because we believe it is; it is true because it is. Many discoveries have verified Jesus' presence on earth, His apostles, and the lands where He lived and preached, which you can visit today in Israel. However, Jesus desires more than just acknowledgment of His existence; He wants you to follow His example and be with Him forever. He wants your heart. Jesus said He is the way, the truth, and the life, and that no one comes to the Father except through Him, and this is made clear with the more than one hundred verses in the Bible that state that Jesus is the only way to God the Father.

Understanding truth is crucial because your eternity is at stake. Learn to differentiate ice cream from insulin, subjective preferences from objective reality. Live in the objective biblical truth of Jesus' teachings, and that truth will set you free (John 8:32).

Sources:
- McDowell, S. (2024). Retrieved from https://seanmcdowell.org/
- Dr. Frank Turek (2024). Retrieved from https://crossexamined.org/dr-frank-turek/

CHAPTER 26

BE A GOOD LISTENER

"People don't listen to understand; they listen to reply."
— STEPHEN R. COVEY, AUTHOR/EDUCATOR

If you want to make better connections with others, then become a better listener. It is one of the simplest strategies in the world. Now, I said *simple*, not *easy*. The key? Shut your mouth and open your ears. This is not a new problem. Epictetus, the Greek philosopher who lived 55-135 AD, said, "We have two ears and one mouth so we can listen twice as much as we speak." Yet, so many people in the world are desperate to be heard. However, everyone is trying to get their two cents in and no one is listening.

To be a better listener, you must be present and engaged. Set down your phone. Take your AirPods out and look the other person in the eye. Give them your full attention, and then just listen. You will be tempted to butt into the conversation and begin to tell them about yourself or share a story about something that happened to you. Instead, just listen. Listen to understand their point of view. Listen to understand their worries or even their problems.

Another strategy you can implement to become a better listener is to ask a follow-up question or a clarity question. For example, "So, am I understanding you right when you said,_____?" or "Tell me more about this." If you can discipline yourself to truly listen at this level, you will be amazed at the deep connections you will make.

As best-selling author Bryant McGill said, "One of the most sincere forms of respect is actually listening to what another has to say."

Nic's Notes —

To become a great communicator, start by becoming a great listener. The truth is, you learn nothing by speaking, only by listening. In my experience, the times when I have had the greatest impact on someone were when they truly felt heard. It wasn't about what I said or did; rather, it was simply the act of listening.

There will be times when you catch yourself forming a response in your head while the other person is talking. Resist this urge and re-engage in listening. As Mark LeBlanc wisely said, "The greatest gift we can give to another person is the gift of listening."

This kind of focused listening, often called "active listening," not only helps you understand others better but also fosters deeper connections and trust. When people believe they are heard, they feel valued. So, focus on *truly listening. You will find that your communication skills naturally improve, allowing you to make a more meaningful impact on those around you.*

Journal & Discussion
Consider these questions, then journal your thoughts, ideas, and insights.

1. Why do you think it is important to listen carefully to someone when they are speaking?

___

2. Can you think of a time when someone interrupted you during a conversation because they wanted to talk? How did that make you feel?

___

3. Have you ever felt heard and listened to? How did that make you feel?

___

4. How can becoming a better listener help you become a better student?

_____

_____

_____

_____

5. What small step can you take today to become a better listener?

_____

_____

_____

_____

CHAPTER 27

Lead by Example

"Leading by example is the most powerful advice you can give to anybody."
— N.R. Narayana Murthy, Indian businessman

People are watching you — observing how you handle stress, perform under pressure, and navigate the influence of peers. They're noticing if you follow the wrong crowd or stand up for what's right, even when it is unpopular. Every action you take is being observed by someone.

The adults are watching — your parents, coaches, and especially your teachers. But mostly, your friends are watching closely, gauging your actions before deciding their own.

Lead by example. Be someone whom other parents would gladly want their children to follow.

How do you achieve this?

- **Excel in your classes.** Resist the temptation to merely scrape by. Building a successful life requires more. Refrain from cheating, even if it seems like everyone else is doing it. Show respect to your teachers and classmates. Such respect is always a wise investment.

- **Own up to your mistakes.** Admit when you mess up or forget an assignment. Crafting lame excuses will not earn you any favors. However, honesty will earn respect.

- **Engage in school activities.** Whether it is sports, music, or clubs, participation matters more than being the star player. Simply being involved speaks volumes.

- **Maintain a positive attitude**, even when faced with doing something you do not like. Choosing optimism in challenging circumstances reveals strong character.

- **Practice kindness.** In a world riddled with hate, choose to be compassionate, even in the face of mistreatment or misunderstanding. Society needs more individuals like you, who courageously embrace kindness.

Nic's Notes —

A couple of years ago, after delivering a keynote speech to a large group in Chicago, a man about sixty years old approached me and said, "You were on my flight this morning." Surprised, I responded, "Oh, really?"

He continued, "Yes, you switched seats with a passenger so they could sit by their child. I appreciated that about you."

I had no idea anyone had noticed. What if I had refused? What if I had been selfish? What if I had agreed to switch but made a fuss or acted reluctantly? This experience made me more aware of my actions and responses going forward. You never know who is watching or how your behavior might impact others. Every action, no matter how small, can leave a lasting impression. Strive to act with kindness and consideration, even when you think no one is watching. Your actions speak volumes about your character and can inspire others in unexpected ways.

Journal & Discussion

Consider these questions, then journal your thoughts, ideas, and insights.

1. What qualities do you think are important for someone to lead by example?

_____
_____
_____
_____

2. Actions speak louder than words. What does that mean to you?

_____
_____
_____
_____

3. Do you know someone who says one thing and does another? How does that make you feel?

_____

_____

_____

_____

4. Have you ever caught someone being kind to someone and they didn't realize you noticed? How did that affect their reputation in your eyes?

_____

_____

_____

_____

5. What steps can you take to better lead by example?

_____

_____

_____

_____

CHAPTER 28

BE BRAVE

"Courage is being scared to death but saddling up anyway."
— John Wayne, Hollywood actor

Throughout life, there are countless moments when bravery becomes essential. Whether that means navigating conflicts with friends or standing up to authority figures, these instances demand courage. It is about choosing to confront challenges rather than shrinking away from them.

Drawing inspiration from the Bible, we find numerous examples of individuals who exemplified bravery. Consider David, who fearlessly faced the towering Goliath when others trembled with fear. Esther risked her life by approaching the king without an invitation, driven by her commitment to her people. Daniel's steadfast faith led him to defy persecution, even in the face of a den full of hungry lions. And Moses, with unwavering resolve, confronted the pharaoh to secure the liberation of his people from bondage.

In our own lives, we will also have opportunities to demonstrate bravery. It might mean standing up to a bully, advocating for us or others, or challenging societal injustices. The decision to be brave is one that each person must face, and it will test our courage and resolve.

In the midst of adversity, choosing bravery can feel daunting. However, it is a decision that empowers us to assert our dignity and self-worth. By embracing bravery, we pave the way for positive change, both in our own lives and in the world around us.

So, when faced with the choice to stand up or remain silent, remember the courageous figures from history and Scripture. Let their examples guide you as you navigate life's challenges with bravery and resilience.

Nic's Notes —

It's easy to tell someone to be brave, but actually doing so is entirely different. Courage comes in many forms and exists within all of us. The good news is that you don't need to be brave twenty-four hours a day. In most situations, you only need three seconds of courage to accomplish great things.

As a boy, you might need just three seconds of courage to ask a girl out. As a girl, you might need even less time to say "yes" or "no." It only takes three seconds of courage to ask for help with your homework or a project. If you need to stand up to a bully or stand up for someone else, three seconds of courage will get the job done. As an adult, whether you want to ask for a job, a raise, or a better position, you won't need courage all day long. Three seconds will be enough.

If you believe that you don't have three seconds of courage, borrow it from me, because I believe in you. I don't even need to know you personally to know that you can do brave things with just three seconds of courage.

Journal & Discussion

Consider these questions, then journal your thoughts, ideas, and insights.

1. Can you think of a time when you did something courageous? What was the outcome? How did it make you feel?

___

___

___

___

2. Why is it important to stand up for what you believe in, even if it is difficult?

___

___

___

___

3. Who is someone you admire for their bravery? What can you learn from them?

_____

_____

_____

_____

4. Do you consider yourself a courageous person? Why or why not?

_____

_____

_____

_____

5. What small step can you take today to become more courageous?

_____

_____

_____

_____

Be Brave . . . But for Whom?

Having courage and being brave can take many forms. You might hear incredible stories of bravery from the military, such as the story of Army Specialist Ross A. McGinnis, who received the Medal of Honor posthumously for his act of throwing himself onto a grenade to save the lives of four fellow soldiers in Iraq. Or consider the mother in Zimbabwe who risked her life to save her three-year-old son from a crocodile. Despite sustaining serious injuries, the boy and his mother survived, thanks to her bravery.

There are countless examples of bravery. This kind of courage doesn't always involve risking life and limb. It can also mean risking a friendship or social status by helping someone else. Standing up to a bully, sitting with an "outcast" at the school lunch table, or choosing to follow Christ's example instead of conforming to cultural norms requires incredible bravery. Standing up or intervening on behalf of others is a noble, even biblical, act. Jesus himself said there is no greater love than laying down one's life for another.

You can also be brave for yourself. If you have ever played a sport, spoken in front of others, or participated in a music competition, you have had to be brave. Maybe learning to swim or riding a roller coaster is scary for you; these also require bravery. Even though these fun activities are not necessarily heroic, they require courage. Courage is a conscious action — you push yourself forward when risk or negative emotions encourage you to stay put. In other words, you feel fear or nervousness, but you act anyway.

But what about being brave for God? Many have been killed for their faith, voluntarily suffering death rather than renouncing their Christian beliefs. These brave individuals are called "martyrs." According to Open Doors, a nonprofit organization that monitors persecution against Christians, more than thirteen Christians are killed every day for their faith. Open Doors' 2021 World Watch List report also stated that:

- 12 Christian buildings or churches are attacked daily;
- 12 Christians are imprisoned or unjustly arrested daily;
- 5 Christians are abducted daily;
- 309 million Christians live in places with "extreme" or "very high" levels of persecution; and,
- 1 in 8 Christians worldwide face persecution.

It's one thing to risk your life to save a family member or friend, but to die simply for loving and serving Jesus Christ is courage on another level. One of the most profound accounts of martyrdom comes from East Asia in the 1950s where Pastor Kim and twenty-seven members of his congregation in North Korea paid the ultimate sacrifice when they were killed for their faith.

Consider Jesus' disciples: Even though they were crucified, stoned, stabbed, dragged, skinned, and burned, every apostle of Jesus proclaimed his resurrection until their dying breath, refusing to recant under pressure from the authorities. Their commitment to Jesus' resurrection can help give us confidence in the Gospel. After all, who would die for a cause that they knew to be false?

Being brave not only means standing true in the face of hardship, but it also means defending and proclaiming the truth.

Proclaiming the truth is not about being aggressive or proving that you're right. Today, speaking the truth means bravely going against dominant cultural narratives (also known as "lies") that are destroying lives. Telling the truth means defending the gospel, human life, biblical doctrine, and the most vulnerable members of society.

The good news is that you never have to be courageous or brave by yourself. God has promised that He is with us always (Joshua 1:9). God said He will help us, strengthen us, and hold us in His mighty hand (Isaiah 41:10-13); He will give us power (2 Timothy 1:7); He will not forsake us (1 Chronicles 28:20); He is for us (Romans 8:31), and He will never be shaken. With God on our side, we have no need to fear. So be brave. Be brave for yourself, be brave for others, and be brave for God.

Sources:
- Stonestreet, S. (2011). "Martyrs Hanged and Steamrolled." *Stone the Preacher*, https://stonethepreacher.com/martyrs-hanged-steamrolled/.
- Raypole, C. (2024). "9 Ways to Be Braver." *Psych Central*, https://psychcentral.com/health/ways-to-be-braver#takeaway.
- Hazen, C. (2013). "Did the Apostles Really Die as Martyrs for Their Faith?" *Biola Magazine*. https://www.biola.edu/blogs/biola-magazine/2013/did-the-apostles-really-die-as-martyrs-for-their-f.
- "13 Christians Killed Daily." (2024). *Open Doors*, https://www.opendoorsus.org/en-US/stories/13-christians-killed-day-average/#:~:text=On%20average%2C%20more%20than%2013,roughly%205%2C000%20people%20each%20year.

CHAPTER 29

DEVELOP SELF-CONTROL

"Self-control is strength. Right thought is mastery. Calmness is power."
— JAMES ALLEN, BRITISH AUTHOR

How well have you developed self-control in your life? Can you effectively manage your emotions, actions, and words? When faced with disappointment, do you maintain composure or resort to childish outbursts?

Within each of us, a struggle exists between our desires (what feels good) and our conscience (what we know is right). It becomes evident when someone is driven solely by their desires. They do what feels good to them at that moment, acting impulsively, as if controlled by external forces. Prison populations are largely comprised of individuals lacking self-control.

James 1:19-20 advises us to "let every person be quick to hear, slow to speak, slow to anger; for the anger of man does not produce the righteousness of God." This verse emphasizes the importance of restraint in our daily lives. Focus your attention on the word "daily" here because self-control is cultivated over time.

In reality, adversity is inevitable. People may mistreat, deceive, steal from, or even abuse you. The true test lies in retaining self-control, especially in the face of injustice.

Resist peer pressure to experiment with drugs or engage in other harmful behaviors. Refrain from spreading rumors about others or consuming pornography. It's challenging because sin masquerades as pleasure, but it conceals danger. Do what's right, especially when no one is watching.

If you develop self-control, you will lead a life you can take pride in.

Nic's Notes —

A child lacks self-control. When uncomfortable, they cry; when hungry, they get mad; and when they don't get their way, they throw tantrums. This behavior is expected from a child, but as we grow older, our ability to handle life's circumstances should mature.

Have you ever seen an adult throw a tantrum because they didn't get their way? Don't be like that. Grow up and develop self-control. Learning to handle discomfort and frustration with grace and composure is a true mark of maturity and strength.

Developing self-control not only reflects personal growth but also earns the respect of others and contributes to a more harmonious environment. By managing *your emotions and reactions, you demonstrate emotional intelligence and foster better relationships. Remember, it's through facing challenges calmly and thoughtfully that we truly are mature.*

Journal & Discussion

Consider these questions, then journal your thoughts, ideas, and insights.

1. Why is self-control important in order to lead a successful life?

___

2. How can a lack of self-control lead you down the wrong path?

___

3. How do you think self-control can foster better relationships with your family, teachers, and friends?

4. What are some benefits to having self-control in both your academic and personal life?

_____

_____

_____

_____

5. What one decision can you make today to gain more self-control in your life?

_____

_____

_____

_____

CHAPTER 30

Choose God's Way

*"Many are the plans in the mind of a man,
but it is the purpose of the Lord that will stand."*
— Proverbs 19:21

One of the greatest battles in a person's life is the struggle between the flesh and the spirit. Our sinful nature often clings to our own ways, hindered by pride, steering us away from God's intended path. Too frequently, we prioritize ourselves and what we want for our lives instead of fulfilling God's purpose for us.

Amid life's struggles, you will find yourself torn between many options. Can I just give you the answer upfront? Choose God's path. Rather than contemplating what you want, ask God about the direction He wishes for you. Seek Him in significant life decisions, as well as the small.

If you find yourself lacking courage, seek it from God. If you are searching for direction, turn to Him. Perhaps you are pondering your purpose on this earth. Ask Him and listen carefully.

Often, we wait until our plans fail, leaving us flat on our faces, before seeking our Creator's guidance. Do not turn to God as a last resort. Approach Him first, whether it is about significant matters or trivial ones. Whether you have misplaced a stack of homework or your ChapStick, seek God's assistance. You will be amazed to find them in places you had previously searched fruitlessly.

Seek God earnestly, making Him your primary focus in every aspect of life.

Nic's Notes —

Proverbs 19:21 states, "Many are the plans in a man's heart, but it's the Lord's purpose that prevails." One of the most famous stories about resisting God's plan is that of the prophet Jonah. Despite knowing what God wanted him to do, Jonah chose his own path. Consequently, he spent three days and three nights in the belly of a whale. In the end, Jonah followed God's plan anyway.

My advice: Save yourself the trouble and the unpleasant experience of a whale's belly by doing it God's way the first time.

Journal & Discussion

Consider these questions, then journal your thoughts, ideas, and insights.

1. Can you think of a time when you resisted following God's lead? If so, what happened?

_____

_____

_____

_____

2. Are you tempted to do life your way instead of God's way? Why or why not?

_____

_____

_____

_____

3. What can happen if you ignore God's lead in your life?

_____

_____

_____

_____

4. Is there anything getting in the way of you seeking God in your life?

_____

_____

_____

_____

5. What steps can you take to be more deliberate about seeking God in your life?

_____

_____

_____

_____

_____

_____

_____

_____

_____

_____

_____

_____

Be Thankful for Unanswered Prayers

This is a true story (with names changed to protect anonymity).

Beth was a typical teenager in high school. She came from a good home, had a younger sister and lots of friends at school. She was an average student and enjoyed basketball, although she was only an average athlete. Beth was a sweet girl, well-liked by her peers and teachers, but not exceptionally popular. Despite being pretty, she didn't think she was because she didn't attract much attention from boys. She had boys who were friends, but not a boyfriend. She was, however, very active in her church and youth group, earning her the label of a "good girl." As one boy told her, "You're the kind of girl a boy wants to marry, not date." What does that even mean? Because of her good-girl reputation, she was never invited to Saturday night parties at the barn, where drinking and hanging out without adult supervision were typical. Even if she had been invited, Beth would not have gone, knowing it wasn't a place that glorified God. Still, many of the boys she liked were there.

One of those boys was Kevin. Kevin was the quarterback of the football team, the point guard on the basketball team, a track star, super popular, cute, funny, and he drove a completely restored 1969 Camaro. It's like he was straight out of a movie. Of course, Beth wasn't the only one who wanted to date Kevin. In fact, most girls did, even those from other schools.

While their reputations differed greatly, Beth and Kevin were friends and did hang out in the same friend group. She hoped and prayed that one day he would see her differently and that they could be more than friends. In fact, she prayed every night for God to bring her and Kevin together for a "happily ever after." Beth crushed on Kevin for almost two years, and she finally confessed her feelings before they graduated. She left a heartfelt note on his windshield, baring her soul. There was no turning back now.

Kevin read the note and later found Beth. He said those dreaded words: "I just want to be friends." She had heard it all before: "I like you, but not like that;" "I don't want to ruin our friendship;" "You're too good for me;" and "You're so nice, you can have any guy you want." It was all rejection, but in different words. Beth was crushed. She and Kevin would remain friends, but nothing more. Beth often wondered why God never answered her prayers for a relationship with Kevin. She wanted to be happy like every other girl, wearing Kevin's class ring and letter jacket. But it never happened for Beth in high school, and she wondered if it ever would.

Kevin went on to marry the head cheerleader. Predictably, he went to college, became a big-time insurance salesman, and made a lot of money. He and his wife settled back in their hometown, where he built a huge, beautiful home with an in-ground pool. They had three children who seemed destined to follow in their parents' footsteps: beautiful and athletic. They went to church every Sunday, and Kevin played golf every Saturday at the best local course, where he was a member. But all wasn't as perfect as it seemed. Kevin had a secret, and it was a big one. He had a dark side, broke the law in various ways, and was eventually found out and sent to prison.

He lost everything. His wife divorced him, and he lost custody of his kids when he went to jail. His big house had to be sold, and his wife and kids moved in with her parents in a small, cramped house. His destroyed reputation spilled onto his family, and his kids had to move to another school. His ex-wife and kids even changed their last name to distance themselves further from him.

Beth had a front-row seat to all of this. She was so sad for Kevin's family and victims, and she wondered how something so devastating could have happened. But then she thought, "Thank you, God. Thank you for saying 'no' when I was begging you for a life with Kevin." Beth went on to marry a man who was not at all like "high school" Kevin, but he was actually way better. He was sweet, fun, smart and, most importantly, loved Beth deeply. He led his household as a godly man should. They had two children and lots of adventures, which continue to this day, about thirty years later.

But this isn't just a story about the dangers of sin and how it can destroy lives. This is also a story about our Heavenly Father. God is omnipotent, omnipresent, and omniscient — all-powerful, always present, and all-knowing. He is not bound by time or place. He knows everything, from the beginning to the end. God knew what choices Kevin would make in his life. He knew the future that Beth would have had if she had married him. But because Beth was praying to God and seeking His plan and not her own, He guided her in a different direction. This is a real-life example of Proverbs 3:5-6, which states: "Trust in the Lord with all your heart and lean not on your own understanding; in all your ways acknowledge Him, and He will direct your path."

When you pray and petition God for the desires of your heart, He will answer, but it may not be the answer you want. Sometimes God says "yes," sometimes He says "no," and other times He commands us to wait. Regardless, if we trust Him and remember that He knows infinitely more than we do and loves us infinitely more than we can understand, we can more easily follow His path and not our own. We all have tried to blaze our own trail, and hopefully we have quickly realized that it leads us to a dangerous place. Stay in God's Word, pray, seek His direction, and trust Him, no matter what.

Sources:

https://www.cogwriter.com/god-omnipotent-omniscient-omnipresent.htm

CHAPTER 31

BUILD BETTER RELATIONSHIPS

*"Success in life depends on the support
and quality of your relationships."*
— JOHN C. MAXWELL, AMERICAN AUTHOR/PASTOR

If you want to unlock the doors of opportunity in life, focus on building positive relationships. This is not about popularity but about forming genuine connections with people who share your mindset.

When others like you, they tend to do two things. First, they offer encouragement. We naturally cheer on those we like, pushing them to try new things, join a team or club, or improve a skill or meet new people. Second, they give opportunities to those they like. In the professional world, bosses often offer more chances to employees they like, such as extra training, additional work hours for extra cash, or even a shot at a management position because they see potential.

Whether we like it or not, success in life often hinges on the relationships we build. You could be the most skilled worker in your company, but if you cannot get along with others, you will end up job-hunting sooner than you would think.

So, commit to improving your people skills and you will find doors opening up for you. Here are a few tips to help you get better at it: Be friendly and approachable, smile often, show interest in others by asking about them and truly listen for their response, avoid talking about yourself too much, focus on being positive instead of negative, and strive to be someone whom others can rely on. Give these a try and see what happens!

Nic's Notes —

Almost every significant door that has opened for me in my career has been the result of a relationship. The truth is, I was ready to quit and find a new career, but someone liked me enough to encourage me to keep going. Along my journey, someone else believed in me enough to offer an opportunity I probably didn't deserve or wasn't ready for, but they did it anyway. Those words of encouragement and those opportunities led to new relationships, which in turn opened even more doors.

You can be the absolute best at what you do, but if no one can work with you or stand to be around you, failure will be inevitable. Focus on building strong relationships and watch the doors of opportunity open for you.

Journal & Discussion

Consider these questions, then journal your thoughts, ideas, and insights.

1. What are some ways that relationships can open doors in the future for you?

_____
_____
_____
_____

2. By not having good relationships with others, how will doors in your future close?

_____
_____
_____
_____

3. How can building better relationships help you better serve your friends and family?

_____
_____
_____
_____

4. What are some skills you can develop that will help you build better relationships with others?

___

___

___

___

5. Who is someone you know that is great at building relationships? What can you learn from watching them?

___

___

___

___

CHAPTER 32

TAKE PRIDE IN WHAT YOU DO

"If you're going to do something, do it with pride."
— UNKNOWN

Do you take pride in what you do? Taking pride in what you do entails feeling a deep sense of satisfaction and accomplishment, regardless of the size or perceived importance of the task at hand.

Your level of pride in your performance should not change based on the perceived significance of your actions. Put simply, even if you believe that your task or position is not important, you should still strive to excel in it. This is not just a good idea, but it is a biblical truth. Colossians 3:23 says, "Whatever you do, work at it with all your heart, as working for the Lord, not for human masters."

I know a young man who took immense pride in the simple task of picking up the kickoff tee during football games. When our team kicked off to start a series, this young man dashed onto the field with a sense of urgency and determination rarely seen in other players. He truly took pride in his role. It would have been easy for him to dismiss his job as unimportant because he wasn't the quarterback or star linebacker, but he understood the value of taking pride in his work.

Do you take pride in everything you do? Whether it is a work-study job or an after-school job, do you strive to complete your tasks to the best of your ability? Are your school projects approached with a high level of pride, or do you simply go through the motions? During sports or music practice, do you take pride in your work and give your best effort, or do you merely do the minimum required to get by?

You may not currently hold the position or role you aspire to, but taking pride in everything you do can yield unexpected results. Do your best where God has placed you. Remember, everything is just a test.

Nic's Notes —

There's a story I love about a janitor who worked at NASA during the 1960s. When President John F. Kennedy visited NASA's Space Center, he saw a janitor carrying a broom and walked over to him. The president asked, "What are you doing?" The janitor replied, "I'm helping put a man on the moon." This janitor saw his work as an integral part of the larger mission, and he took pride in contributing to that mission.

Take pride in everything you do. Your work—whether on the field, court, or in the classroom—represents not only you but also all those who sacrificed so you can have the life you lead today.

Journal & Discussion

Consider these questions, then journal your thoughts, ideas, and insights.

1. What does taking pride in your work mean to you? Why is that important?

___

___

___

___

2. What is something you have accomplished that you are particularly proud of? What in particular made you feel that way?

___

___

___

___

3. What role does self-discipline and perseverance play in creating something you can be proud of?

___

___

___

___

4. How do you feel when you put your best effort into something regardless of the outcome?

_____

_____

_____

_____

5. What would you tell someone who believes their best is not good enough or does not matter? How would you encourage them?

_____

_____

_____

_____

CHAPTER 33

ASK YOURSELF THE RIGHT QUESTIONS

"At the end of the day, the questions we ask ourselves determine the type of people that we will become."
— LEO BABAUTA, JOURNALIST/AUTHOR

The questions you ask yourself are like seeds you plant for your future. If you plant negative questions, you will harvest negative thoughts. Take this question, for example: "Why don't I get any playing time on the basketball team?" Once you ask this, your brain will start churning out negative reasons like, "Because the coach doesn't like me," or "because I am too short, or "because no one but my mom sees my potential." These thoughts aren't helpful at all.

On the flip side, if you plant positive questions, you will reap positive responses. Consider asking, "What could I do to become a better basketball player?" Watch how your brain springs into action, offering suggestions like, "I can get in better shape;" "I can work on becoming a better ball handler;"

"I can improve my shooting;" "I can improve my attitude." And the list goes on.

Changing your mindset from negative to positive can work wonders.

It might be tempting to sit back and wait for others to notice your talents or invest in you, but that is not the best approach. Instead, cultivate a habit of asking yourself positive questions. This will equip you to seize opportunities and navigate life's challenges effectively. So, plant the seeds of positivity in your mind, and then watch them grow into a bright future.

Nic's Notes —

The difference between these two questions is a difference in action and responsibility. The negative questions put the other person in the driver's seat and make you out to be the victim. Positive questions put you in the driver's seat and set you up to be an instrument of change.

It's easy to feel like a victim or to think someone is treating you unfairly. The truth is, you might be right, but that won't change your circumstances. This world is unfair and broken, but you still get to choose to be in the driver's seat of your life. Unfair and unequal things will happen to you, but only you can decide how to respond. You can either play the victim and blame others for your circumstances or you can strive to make yourself better. This choice will hinge on the questions you ask yourself. Work on yourself and choose to become better at whatever it is you do.

Actor and comedian Steve Martin said, "Be so good they can't ignore you."

Journal & Discussion

Consider these questions, then journal your thoughts, ideas, and insights.

1. How important is self-talk in your success?

_____
_____
_____
_____

2. How do you speak to yourself when you make a mistake? Positively or negatively? Why?

_____
_____
_____
_____

3. What can you do to take any negative self-talk out of your vocabulary?

_____
_____
_____
_____

4. What can you do to become more aware of the questions you ask yourself?

_____
_____
_____
_____

5. What are some positive questions you can ask yourself on a regular basis?

Daring Dreams vs. Daydreams: The Path to Purposeful Achievement

John C. Maxwell, a renowned leadership expert, draws a crucial distinction between "daring dreams" and "daydreams," highlighting the importance of purposeful ambition over idle fantasies. This concept is from his book, *Dare to Dream ... Then Do It*. Understanding the difference between these two lines of thought can significantly impact your level of success in your personal and professional life.

You have more control over your future than you may think. Too often, however, we hand that control over to chance. We wish upon a falling star, hoping something great will happen to us, when instead we should roll up our sleeves and get to work. The difference lies between a daydream and a daring dream.

Daydreams are nothing more than mere wishes — things you want but are not necessarily working to achieve. You can even want them a lot, but they remain daydreams if the action is not there.

A daring dream, too, is something you want, but the difference is that you get up each day and work for it.

Here's a list of distinctions between daring dreams and daydreams, mostly taken from Maxwell's book.

Daring Dream	Daydream
Relies on discipline	Relies on luck
Focuses on the journey	Focuses on the destination
Encourages you to take action	Encourages you to be lazy
Maximizes the value of hard work	Minimizes the value of hard work
Leads to action	Leads to excuses
Creates momentum	Creates inertia
Breeds teamwork	Breeds isolation
Initiates	Waits
Embraces risk as necessary	Avoids all risks
Relies on your efforts	Relies on the efforts of others
Requires 100% personal responsibility	Blames others

You don't have to look far to find someone staking their entire future on a daydream. A perfect example is someone who sees their future determined by winning the lottery or discovering they have a rich uncle who just left them their entire inheritance.

Another example of a daydreamer is someone who wishes they could be a star basketball player without ever playing. They may sit and dream about hitting the game-winning three-pointer or dunking the ball right over the opposing team's star player. They can hear the crowd cheer as the buzzer goes off and the team wins the championship. But they never join the team.

A daring dream may look very similar on the surface, but the difference lies in the execution. A person with a daring dream may also dream of hitting the winning three-pointer or dunking the ball, but they get up each day and put in the hard work. They shoot five hundred extra shots each practice and practice in the off-season with drills and workouts to improve their vertical. The daring dreamer and the daydreamer both have the same dream, but one has a much greater chance of seeing their dream become a reality.

What kind of dreams are filling your thoughts? Are they daring dreams or are they just daydreams? Here is the truth: Most of us have some daydreams. The challenge is to turn those daydreams into daring dreams. If you are wondering how to do that, the answer lies in the word "action." You must put some action into your daydreams for them to become daring dreams.

I challenge you to search your heart for a daring dream that God has placed there and pursue it with everything you have. Daring dreams have the ability to unlock your potential and set you on a path toward a more fulfilling and successful life.

Source:
Maxwell, J. C. (2006). *Dare to dream ... then do it: What successful people know and do.* Thomas Nelson, Inc.

CHAPTER 34

Find a Mentor

*"One of the greatest values of mentors
is the ability to see ahead what others cannot see
and to help them navigate a course to their destination."*
— John C. Maxwell

A mentor is more than just a friend. They are someone who really cares about you and wants to see you do well in school, in life, and in your future career. For students like you, growing up and figuring out what you want to do can be tough. That is when a mentor comes in handy. They are like a wise friend you can talk to about anything, from homework stress to problems with friends.

Mentors can be anyone, from teachers and coaches to family friends or people in your community. What makes them special is that they have been through similar things and can give you advice based on their own experiences. They have learned a lot along the way, and they want to share their experiences with you to help you avoid making the mistakes that they made.

Having a mentor also means having someone to look up to, someone who believes in you and encourages you to do your best. They are like your personal cheerleader, cheering you on when things get tough and celebrating your successes, no matter how small.

So, if you are a student looking for someone to help you navigate through the ups and downs of growing up, consider finding a mentor. They can be the support you need to reach your full potential and achieve your dreams.

Nic's Notes —

I have had several mentors in my life. Some of my teachers, coaches, and even a past superintendent have mentored me. I have mentors in my professional career, and each of these individuals has guided and directed me throughout my life and career. They have offered advice and introduced me to key relationships. They have steered me away from mistakes and kept me out of harm's way. I've often asked myself, "Why do they do it? What's in it for them?"

As I have become a mentor to others, I realize why they do it. It's because mentors can. It's because they want to help and be a part of something bigger than themselves. They invest in others because someone invested in them. The satisfaction of seeing someone else grow and succeed, partly because of their guidance, is a powerful motivator.

> Mentorship is a cycle of giving and receiving, a way to pay forward the help one has received. It's about creating a legacy of support and growth. So, find a mentor. Seek out someone who can guide you, challenge you, and help you navigate your journey.

Journal & Discussion

Consider these questions, then journal your thoughts, ideas, and insights.

1. Do you have someone in your life whom you trust that will mentor you and give you advice?

___

2. How can having a mentor contribute to your personal and professional growth and success?

___

3. What qualities would you like to see in a mentor?

_____

_____

_____

_____

_____

4. Whom do you know that could be a good mentor to you?

_____

_____

_____

_____

5. What steps could you take to find someone who could mentor you?

_____

_____

_____

_____

CHAPTER 35

Invest in Yourself

"You will be the same person in five years as you are today except for the people you meet and the books you read."
— Charlie "Tremendous" Jones, author/inspirational speaker

What skills would you like to master? What are you doing to improve yourself? I know you are in school and constantly consuming information, but what else are you doing?

What skills are you learning outside the classroom? What books are you reading, and what podcasts are you listening to? How are you spending your free time? Are you building skills and acquiring knowledge that will make you more valuable as an adult, or are you just wasting time? If you are spending your free time reading surface-level novels, playing video games, or scrolling on social media, are you putting a time limit on it? I am not saying those activities are bad, but I'm not saying they are good, either. Countless people have lost their way because they did not have a plan for balancing enjoyment and growth.

Author and CEO Jeb Blount said, "If you do not have a plan, you will become part of someone else's plan. You can either take control of your life, or someone else will use you to enhance theirs. It's your choice."

To determine if a hobby is making you better or just wasting your time, consider these simple questions:

- Are you learning a new skill or gaining knowledge that will be helpful in life?
- Is it aiding in stress relief or giving you joy and satisfaction?
- Are you meeting new people or strengthening relationships?
- Does it promote overall health and well-being?
- Are you using this hobby to procrastinate other important tasks?
- Is it taking up a reasonable amount of your time, or does this hobby consume you?

You only get twenty-four hours in a day. How you spend them will help determine where you go in life.

Nic's Notes —

I know more people than I can list who have changed their lives by investing in themselves. I know real-estate multimillionaires and business owners who learned the ins and outs of their fields by reading and making friends. I know certified welders who learned their skill in their garage in their free time by watching YouTube videos. I know computer programmers who learned what they know from trial and error. What do all these people have in common? They all invested in themselves. They didn't wait for someone to pay them to learn. They took initiative, were willing to fail, and started learning in small ways.

As the Chinese proverb says, "The journey of a thousand miles begins with a single step."

Start walking today.

Journal & Discussion

Consider these questions, then journal your thoughts, ideas, and insights.

1. **What are some goals or dreams you have for your future, and how can investing in yourself help you achieve them?**

___

2. **How do you currently use your free time, and how could you better use some of that free time to start investing in yourself?**

___

3. Make a list of ways you can invest in yourself. It could be in academics, sports, music, or something completely different.

___

___

___

___

4. Is there any skill or discipline you wish you had? What is stopping you from learning that skill or discipline on your own?

___

___

___

___

5. How could your life look different if you started investing in yourself in a more deliberate way?

___

___

___

___

CHAPTER 36

GIVE SOMETHING BACK

"At the end of the day, it's not about what you have or even what you've accomplished — it's about who you've lifted up, who you've made better. It's about what you've given back."
—DENZEL WASHINGTON, ACTOR

This entire curriculum has focused on you — how to set yourself up for success, how to improve, and how to be ready for life. But life isn't solely about you. God has placed you on this earth for a greater purpose than self-service. I want to encourage you to find ways to give back. You are here today because someone invested in you. Someone sacrificed their time, energy, and money so you could thrive. Whom can you invest in? Is there another student in this school whom you could encourage, befriend, or mentor? You possess information and life experiences that others can benefit from if you are willing to share them. Seek someone to share them with.

If you have not already, I urge you to adopt an attitude of service. Become someone who is consistently focused on others. You do not need to be an upperclassman or hold a position of authority to make a difference; you simply need to care and take action.

There is a phrase that resonates: "Each one, reach one." Whom can you reach? Whom can you show the love of Christ to?

Throughout the Bible, Christ demonstrated His love through service. He fed the hungry, clothed the naked, healed the sick, and offered hope to the hopeless. Be an instrument of His love. You can impact someone's life profoundly simply by loving others.

Nic's Notes —

In the previous chapter, I asked you to find a mentor. Now it's time to be a mentor. I understand what you might be thinking: "How can I be someone's mentor when I am trying to figure this out myself?" The beauty of being a mentor is that you don't have to have life completely figured out to help someone else. You don't have to be at the top of the mountain to be a mentor. All you have to be is one small step ahead of someone else in order to reach back and help them along their way.

If you are an upperclassman, you can befriend an underclassman. If you are on the starting lineup, you can help someone who is struggling to make the team. Maybe you are filled with confidence and courage, and you can help someone who might be still looking for that in their life. If you have been in this school system *for a while, you can reach out to the new kid who may feel all alone.*

By reaching out, you may never know the real difference you make in another's life. But reach out anyway. This is not about you. This is about what you can do for someone else.

Journal & Discussion
Consider these questions, then journal your thoughts, ideas, and insights.

1. Think of a time when another student or teacher helped you. How did that make you feel?

_____
_____
_____
_____

2. How can being a mentor to others help you boost your leadership skills and confidence?

_____
_____
_____
_____

3. What skills can you develop to become a better mentor to others?

_____

_____

_____

_____

4. What impact could you have on another person by simply listening to them and being their friend?

_____

_____

_____

_____

5. Whom do you know that could use your help? What could you do to help them?

_____

_____

_____

_____

What *Really* Matters

The news wasn't new to Dave: cancer. Again. This time it was lung cancer. He had beaten colon cancer and skin cancer before with chemotherapy, but this time the look on the doctor's face was different. He glanced at the chart, sat on the stool beside the bed, and gently placed his hand on Dave's shoulder. After a brief pause, he looked up and said, "Dave, there's nothing we can do this time. We've exhausted all our options, and nothing is working. I'm referring you to hospice . . . I am so, so sorry."

Dave couldn't believe his ears. Isn't hospice for people who are dying? Was he dying? As if reading his mind, the doctor added, "You don't have long. Based on these tests, you have maybe three to four months." The doctor left the room, and Dave felt like he was in a movie. His wife, quietly processing the information, gathered the brochures the nurse handed her. This was it, he thought.

Dave went home, and just as the doctor had predicted, within months he was confined to his bed. The cancer was killing him. One day, as he rested with his family around him, Dave quietly slipped away from one life to the next.

At the moment of our deaths, almost nothing matters. It doesn't matter how much money you have, how many vacations you took, or how important you are in this world.

You might argue that it matters to Dave's family — the memories they made and the legacy he left behind — and that's true. But to Dave, those things are of no concern. All that matters to him when he leaves this earth is what he did with Jesus Christ. Is Dave sitting with Jesus in Heaven or not?

It's easy to get distracted by the things of this world: money, popularity, power, and possessions — all of which are temporary. In this digital age, these distractions have multiplied exponentially. People are now obsessed or even addicted to "likes," "comments," and "shares."

Numerous studies show that the earlier the engagement on social media platforms occurs, the more likely there will be changes in the brain — and not in a good way. The pursuit of more "likes" rewires the brain's reward system, driving people to get more "likes" and "comments," perpetuating a never-ending cycle. Ironically, the more one uses social media, the more isolated one feels, leading to increased loneliness and even depression. It's easy to get caught up in the endless cycle of mindless scrolling, commenting, and chasing the high of that dopamine hit. And for what? These are temporary feelings in a temporary world. Set your mind on things that have eternal value.

Your value does not come from any place online. The Creator of all things knits you together in your mother's womb. He loves you, cherishes you, and He is always with you. He loves you so much that He saved you from your sins. Some opinions do not matter, like those of the countless trolls on every social media platform. But the one opinion that matters most is that of your Heavenly Father. Listen to Him, not your "friends" online.

Think about Dave again. Just like it happened to him, death will come to us all. We don't know when or where, but it is a fact of life, and each one of us will face eternity. On that day when we leave our earthly body behind and are present with our Lord and Savior, what really matters? Likes on Instagram? No. Views on TikTok? No. How many followers you had? No. All that will matter is your relationship with Christ and the influence you had on others. Resist the temptation to assign value to things that are not valuable. Instead, treasure what is invaluable. Make the most of every day that God gives you and focus on the eternity ahead with Him!

Final Thoughts

As you reach the end of this book, I hope you've gained more than just knowledge of the thirty-six virtues outlined in the *Life Ready* curriculum. My wish is that you've found guidance, inspiration, and a sense of purpose that will accompany you on your journey through life. Remember, these virtues are not just ideals to strive for — they are practical tools to help you navigate challenges, build meaningful relationships, and create a life that is not only successful but also deeply fulfilling.

The path ahead will have its ups and downs, but you now have a compass to guide you. Keep this book and refer to it often. The ideas and insights you've journaled have the power to change not only your life but also the lives of others. Each virtue represents a step toward becoming the best version of yourself. Use these virtues to shape your actions, influence your decisions and, most importantly, guide you toward a life that you can be proud of.

As you move forward, continue to reflect on these virtues, integrate them into your daily life, and let them transform how you make decisions. Your journey has just begun, and the world is full of opportunities waiting for you to seize.

Thank you for taking the time to explore these virtues with me. Now, go forth with confidence, purpose, and a heart full of compassion for others. The future is yours to create.

About the Author

Throughout his career, **Nic Bittle** has been known not just as a storyteller but as a guide for those seeking to elevate their communication and performance in the workplace. As a professional speaker, author, and host of the *Nic Bittle Life & Leadership* podcast, co-hosted with his spouse, Tarina Bittle, Nic has dedicated his life to helping others reach their full potential. Nic, Tarina, and their two children live in the close-knit community of Corn, Oklahoma — a small town in the heart of America that they proudly call home.

Nic's journey is deeply rooted in Christian education. His parents, Larry and Teresa Bittle, felt a strong calling to provide a Christian learning environment for their children, which led them to establish Victory Christian School in western Oklahoma. Nic and his siblings were among the first students to attend, laying the foundation for a lifelong commitment to faith-based education. After their early years at Victory Christian School, Nic and his siblings continued their education at Corn Bible Academy (CBA), a Christian school with a rich history dating back to 1902.

It was at CBA that Nic met his future wife, Tarina Nikkel. Tarina's connection to the school runs deep, as she became the fourth generation in her family to graduate from CBA. She followed in the footsteps of her great-grandfather, Cornelius Bergman, who was the school's first graduate in 1906. Nic and Tarina's children, Elle and Cruze, will be the fifth generation to carry on this tradition at Corn Bible Academy.

Nic's passion for helping others extends beyond the workplace. In *Life Ready*, he brings the same principles and virtues that have shaped his career to the next generation, guiding students toward a future filled with purpose and success. His hope is that the wisdom shared in this book will not only prepare students for the challenges ahead but also inspire them to lead lives that are both meaningful and fulfilling.

www.ingramcontent.com/pod-product-compliance
Lightning Source LLC
Chambersburg PA
CBHW061820290426
44110CB00027B/2925